Coarse Fishing

an Illustrated
Teach Yourself book

Blenheim Lake with the Grand Bridge in the background

Fishing a Thames backwater

Peter Stone

Illustrated Teach Yourself **Coarse Fishing**

TREASURE PRESS

First published in Great Britain by Brockhampton Press Ltd
(now Hodder & Stoughton Children's Books)

This edition published in 1983 by Treasure Press
59 Grosvenor Street
London W1

Text © 1969, 1977 Peter Stone
Illustrations © 1969, 1977 Hodder & Stoughton Ltd

ISBN 0 907812 38 4

Printed in Singapore

Line drawings by Richard Walker
Drawings of fish by Irene Hawkins
Photographs by the author except where stated

Contents

METRIC MEASUREMENTS

The following approximate equivalents
may help you:

½	inch	=	12.7	mm	1	ounce	=	28.4	gm
2	,,	=	5.1	cm	5	,,	=	141.8	,,
5	,,	=	12.7	,,	8	,,	=	226.8	,,
17	,,	=	43.2	,,	2	lb	=	0.9	kg
4	feet	=	1.2	m	5	,,	=	2.3	,,
50	yds	=	45.7	m	12	,,	=	5.4	,,

Acknowledgments

My thanks are due to Fred J. Taylor for writing the
chapter on Carp and for all his assistance, to Richard Walker
for the diagrams, to Arnold Neave, chemist of Hitchin, for
printing the photographs, to Maureen Trafford
for typing the manuscript, and to Ron Cook for his
assistance with the proofing. Grateful thanks too, to
Peter Drennan, Ian Tolputt, Fred Towns, Tony Fordham,
and Roger Symonds for giving their time to help with
the photographs.
Lastly, but by no means least, to my wife Sue,
who accepts my sport and long hours away from home with
enduring patience, who welcomes my friends to the house
all hours of the day and night and who encourages
me in every possible way. To her, I dedicate this book.

1 Introduction

Belief is widespread that rain and anglers are synony-
mous: when it rains the fish are supposed to bite. Well,
they don't – at least, not often – although rainy conditions
can sometimes lead to good sport.

Rain and sun Tench, for instance, will feed well in drizzly weather,
especially if the air is humid; I have also found bream in
suicidal mood in such conditions. I once took four good
carp in just over an hour, with rain beating into my face.
But although some of the photographs in this book show
either me or my friends fishing in adverse conditions, I
should make it clear that fishing isn't only worthwhile
when the weather is bad. I have caught many big fish in
brilliant sunshine, often with the sun scorching my back,
and whether or not I fish in hot weather depends largely on
the species being sought.

For instance on a July morning, you set out at dawn to
catch some roach. At first light they begin to feed and
continue until the sun rises. As the sun gets higher in the
sky, however, so the bites decrease until they stop completely. Roach fishing will now be poor until evening unless
the water is weedy, when they will continue to feed and
your bait should be among or close to the weed beds. But

The correct way to return
a fish to the water. A
four-pound tench lives to
fight another day

The right way to unhook a big fish. The author with a 4¾-lb. tench

chub will feed no matter how hot the weather, so if you intend staying at the waterside, change tactics and fish for chub. Carp, tench, and rudd are just three other species which feed in hot weather, so you see it is quite possible to fish in glorious weather and still catch good fish. Taking things all round, I prefer the sun to the rain any time.

Photography I am always being asked by non-anglers how on earth I dispose of all the fish that I catch, so let me make the position clear. All the fish photographed in this book were alive and returned to the water to live another day with the exception of the chub and dace on page 92, which I had to kill in order to show the formation of the fins. Photographs of fish have become more popular than stuffed ones during the last decade, and a pictorial record of outstanding catches adds to the enjoyment of reminiscing.

Handling fish When handling fish I do not believe in holding them with a piece of rag. Hold the fish carefully with damp hands and in this way as little damage as possible is done.

Unhooking A great many fish are damaged during the unhooking process. Should the fish be heavy – 1 lb. or over, say – then the best way is to remove it from the landing net to the grass, then lightly but firmly grip it just behind the head, removing the hook as gently and swiftly as you can. Should the hook be deep, remove it with a pair of artery forceps, which are better than the disgorgers sold for the purpose. If, however, you cannot afford a pair of forceps, then buy a disgorger like the one shown, not one with a prong at the end. Forceps are almost essential when dealing with pike.

Disgorger

Close season Coarse fishing ends on 14th March and opens on 16th June, although some still-waters remain open all year. In most waters, however, no fishing between those dates!

A keepnet should be at least 6 feet in length. The author with a 2 lb 3 oz roach

2 Tackle required

The rod I am assuming that for the time being you can only afford one rod, in which case a 'general' rod is the most sensible buy. Without doubt, the best type is fibreglass, which is not only extremely light but very strong.

An 11-foot rod with full stand-off rings should suffice. For pike, carp and eels, however, a second rod, similar but with a stouter action, will be necessary. Two rods may be beyond the reach of novice anglers but I must stress that a rod suitable for roach, chub, and so on will not do for everything. If, therefore, you can only afford one rod, pike, eels, and carp must be forgotten for the time being.

The reel There are two types of reel, the fixed-spool and the centre-pin. The former is the most popular reel in use today and can be obtained with both right- and left-handed winds. Right-handed anglers should use a left-handed reel and vice-versa. Your 'strong' hand is then gripping the rod while playing a fish while the weaker hand is winding. The main feature of the fixed-spool is a slipping clutch which means that, providing the tension is set correctly, a fish while being played, can take line without fear of breakage. To

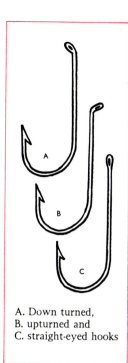

A. Down turned,
B. upturned and
C. straight-eyed hooks

set the clutch, adjust the tension nut, then pull on the line; if the line breaks, then the clutch is set too tight. Slacken off tension until the clutch slips while you are pulling hard on the line, just before the line reaches its maximum breaking strain.

The centre-pin is a drum reel and is extremely free-running. Made from either wood, bakelite, or alloy, it is mounted at its central axis on a steel pivot. These reels are used primarily for 'swimming the stream' (see page 44) and 'stret-pegging' (see page 32). One big advantage is the speed of line recovery, and many top-class match anglers, in order to make this even faster, remove the handles from the reel and then keep tapping the edge of the drum with one hand as rapidly as possibly. This is called 'batting.' One big drawback is that long-distance casting with light leads is difficult, and these reels therefore are not suitable for legering (see page 21).

If you can only afford one reel, then buy a fixed spool. When you are a little more experienced you can, if you want, buy a centre-pin, for both reels have their uses; but if I was limited to one it would be a fixed-spool every time. I would strongly advise having four spools with your reel. You can then wind four different breaking strains of line on them and be equipped for everything. These four should be, 4 lb. b.s., 6 lb. b.s., 8 lb. b.s., and 10 lb. b.s.

The line

The most popular line in use today is Nylon Monofilament, a synthetic line, cheap and easy to knot, and you need look no further than this. There are many makes from which to choose, but whichever one you buy, be sure to get 100 yards, and put all of this on your spool. If you buy under this, say 50 yards, and you lose a lot of line in a snag there will be little left. Test the last few yards of the line before you start fishing, and if any shows signs of weakening (and it often does) break it off. Don't wait until you hook a fish before finding out; it is then too late!

Hooks

These can be bought either tied to lengths of nylon or loose, in which case you tie them yourself.

I use both eyed and ready-tied hooks. As their name implies, eyed hooks have an eye on the end of the shank to which the nylon is attached. Buy only those with the eye straight, i.e. not turned up or down. A wide range of hook sizes will be necessary for all the species you seek ranging from No. 16 to No. 2. For each species you will require the following hook sizes:

Roach: No. 16, 14, 12, 10, and 8.
Bream: No. 12, 10, 8, and 6.
Chub: No. 8, 6, 4, and 2 (No. 16 on rare occasions).
Tench: No. 14, 12, 10, 8, and 6.
Carp: No. 6, 4, and 2.
Perch: No. 12, 10, 8, and 6.
Pike: See Pike chapter: hooks for pike are attached to thin, supple wire.
Barbel: No. 16, 14, 12, 10, 8, and 6.
Eels: No. 6, 4 and 2 (Usually attached to wire).

Landing-net A net on a long handle, used for landing fish when played out. Buy one with a frame 20 inches across. It is very difficult, especially for a beginner, to get a fair-sized fish into a small net. A handle about 8 feet long is advisable, especially for netting a fish off a high bank, or over rushes.

Keepnet A net in which fish are kept alive while the angler continues fishing. As with the landing-net do not buy a small one, as this could cause the death of many fish, especially in summer.

Leger stops These simple but very effective items were introduced several years ago and today are used widely among leger enthusiasts.

The line is passed through a tube approximately ¼ in in length which is then fastened to the line by passing a tapered plastic plug into the tube. The plug should be positioned at the bottom of the tube (the end nearest the hook).

Some tubes are parallel, but the model with a tapered tube introduced by tackle manufacturer Peter Drennan in 1983 is much better.

Plastic Leger Stop

TUBE (¼IN)   PLUG   STOP ATTACHED TO LINE

TO HOOK →

Floats There are hundreds of different types, but you won't need a hundred to go fishing with! For a start, buy some 'Avon' types for river fishing and peacocks for stillwater. Buy four of different shot-loading capacities. As you gain in experience you will add to these but these two patterns will do to start with.

Split shot

Lead For a start get some split shot. Do not buy those little boxes containing about fifteen different sizes, because you rarely require them all. Three sizes will suffice : swan shot (a big split shot, about $\frac{1}{4}$ inch in diameter), B.B., and No. 1. You must also get some leger weights, so ask for Arlesey Bombs. These are a little expensive, but you should have some. Two sizes will do for a start : $\frac{1}{4}$ oz. and $\frac{1}{2}$ oz.

Arlesey Bombs

Tackle carrier You have the choice of a basket, box, or haversack. I prefer a haversack, both for comfort and space. Carrying a box or basket a considerable distance is no joke, as the strap cuts into your shoulder, but straps on a haversack are placed so that the bag rides in the middle of your back.

A haversack for carrying tackle

Stool One disadvantage of a haversack is that you cannot sit on it, but you can buy a lightweight stool which can be strapped to the bag.

Two small, but very important, items remain. A tin of vaseline for greasing the ferrules, and a plummet, a lead with cork in the bottom, for finding the depth of the water.

These, then, are the basic essentials. From time to time you will, no doubt, add to this list, buying another rod or reel, or even an umbrella or a shelter. The latter is only a luxury, but a very welcome one, especially during the winter, when fishing in cold winds and rain. When you acquire other rods you will need a holdall to carry them.

Tackling up In the early stages I advise sticking to float fishing; other methods will come later.

When you arrive at the waterside remove the rod from its bag and put the rod together starting with the top and middle joints. Now place the reel on the handle in line with the rings, about 6 inches from the *top* of the handle; fix it into position with the winch fittings and pull some line off the reel, threading it through the rings. Then pull off about

Assembling the top
and middle joints

Sighting along the rod to
check that the rings are in
alignment

Fixing the reel. This
should be about six inches
from the top of the handle

10 feet of line, and put the rod down where you cannot step on it.

Take a float and remove the rubber band which attaches the float to the line. Then thread the line through the ring at the bottom of the float, and pull the band down on to the float. This fixes it in position. Push the float up the line several feet out of the way. Now attach the lead. If the float carries two split shot, pinch these close together on the line about 16 inches from the end. Finally, take a hook, and attach this to the line. Fix up the landing-net, place unwanted tackle back in the haversack, and decide where you are going to fish. This piece of water is known as the 'swim'.

The next stage is to attach the plummet to the hook. Cast out some distance from where you intend your bait to lie, and gently pull the plummet back into your swim. In this way you are less likely to disturb any fish that may be there. The float may disappear under the surface; if it does, pull it out and push it up the line a couple of feet. Cast again, and if it still disappears, repeat this action, until, with the line taut, the float lies half-cocked on the surface. If it lies flat on the water, it must be pulled down, of course, until half cocked. You now know how deep the swim is, and the float can be set accordingly. Remove the plummet, and you are all ready to start.

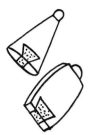

Plummets

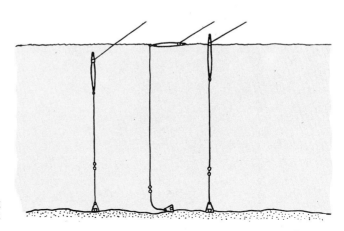

Three stages of plumbing the depth

3 Casting

One does not have to be a good caster to catch fish, but it can be a decided advantage, especially when fishing in narrow, overgrown streams, where the first cast, if not an accurate one will scare the fish. Casting is not difficult to learn, providing you set about it in the right way. To begin with, concentrate on casting from a fixed-spool: the centre-pin can come later.

Casting from a fixed-spool

First make sure that the reel is fixed at the top of your rod handle and use the reel with the handle on the left-hand side. I know this feels the 'wrong way round' to a right-handed angler, but you will soon get used to it. The line should fill the spool to within 1/16 inch of the 'lip', other-wise you cannot cast properly.

Overhead cast

With the right hand, grip the handle immediately below the reel; your fingers will, in fact, be gripping the reel-seat, the part over which the winch-fittings slide, to hold it in position. With the left hand, lift the 'pick-up' (the part of the reel which goes over the spool and which holds the line in position when fishing) and place the middle finger of the right hand on the spool of line. The left hand now grips the rod handle down towards the bottom. The rod is brought back over the shoulder and the cast made. As the bait travels forward, lift the middle finger of the right hand from the spool, slightly dropping the rod top as the bait begins to fall towards the water.

The angler is about to cast. The pick-up is in the 'open' position with the middle finger of the right hand resting against the spool

When the rod is over your shoulder, immediately before casting, do not have too much line hanging from the rod top. If no float is being used, make it about 5 feet and, if using a float, take up the line until the float is some 12 inches from the rod top. It is important that the finger is released from the spool at exactly the right moment, and this will require a little practice.

Underhand cast

This is the cast adopted when legering in narrow, over-grown streams, where accurate casting is essential. Grip the rod with the right hand as before; you won't need your left hand, this being a one-handed cast. Have about a yard of

Left: an overhead cast. Note the bait (circled) on a short line
Right: an underhand cast with the rod held in the right hand only

Making a sideways cast.
Note short line between
rod top and bait (circled)

line hanging, take aim at the desired spot, and swing the bait a couple of times like a pendulum. When you think the aim correct, release your finger from the spool and the bait should land where you want it. When attempting such a cast under trees the inexperienced angler is often inclined to check his tackle in mid-air, thinking that it is going to land in the branches. If you think that, believe me, it will finish up there! When you cast, say to yourself, 'I don't care if it does go in the tree' and cast as if the tree was not there. Nine times out of ten it will go just where you want it to.

Sideways cast This, too, is a one-handed cast, and not always very accurate, but it is useful if you are sitting under trees where an overhead cast is impossible. Again, if possible, have very little line hanging from the rod top.

4 Baits

One could write a book about baits, but there are not many days when a fish cannot be tempted either with maggots, crust, flake or worms, and if you only take these you won't go far wrong. Beginners will find maggots easier to use than bread, but don't feel you have to use them exclusively or spend a lot of money on them.

Paste

Paste is a mixture of stale bread and water and the actual mixing is very important. Most anglers like theirs hard. 'It stays on the hook', they say. But who wants it to stay on? I don't. I want it off, replaced by a fish. Paste must be soft. A fish rejects a hard bait, and I like mine so soft that when I have cast, it comes off on winding the bait back. When it does that the mixture is correct.

Get a loaf a week old, and cut it into slices an inch thick. Hold each slice under a cold-water tap (or in the river) for about three seconds, break it in half and place it in the left hand. With the thumb of your right hand, begin kneading it until it is nice and soft; this takes about three minutes. Do each slice in turn, and then mix the whole lot into a big ball. Give this a further kneading until it is free of lumps, and is very soft. Then put it in a clean bait box until required.

Before mixing, make sure your hands are clean. Do not try to mix paste from a new loaf, because you can't; if the loaf is old enough it will crumble while mixing, and pieces drop out of your hand. Always mix over a clean bowl, picking up the pieces as they drop, reintroducing them into the ball of paste.

Cheese-paste

Another fine bait, and the longer you keep it the better the fish like it, especially chub.

Get some cheese a week old at least, and grate it very fine, making sure it is free of lumps. Place a ball of paste, mixed as described, into a clean bowl, and tip the cheese on top. Mix the two together, adding water if it becomes too hard. The paste, when finished, should be nice and soft. I find that half a pound of cheese, mixed into a loaf, is about right. In a plastic bait box, in a cool place, it will keep for weeks.

Breadcrust For this you require a new loaf. Simply take the loaf with you breaking off pieces off the crust the required size as and when you need them. Some people cut, damp, and press it overnight, but this is entirely unnecessary.

Flake Again take a new loaf, pinch a piece of white from the middle and gently squeeze this round the hook. This is a difficult bait to get used to, but a very effective one.

Lobworms These big garden worms are best gathered after dark, in a damp garden, with the aid of a torch. Tread lightly, grab the worm and pull. A torch with the battery at half power is better than a very bright light.

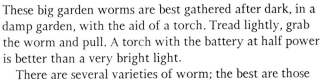

Hooking lobworms

There are several varieties of worm; the best are those with big flat tails. Every fish takes a worm, and when placing it on the hook pass the hook through once. If you keep passing the hook through, you eventually tie the worm in a knot, and a fish does not expect to see a worm doing contortions! Worms are best kept in a box in wet sacking and leaves, or simply earth, away from the sun. Don't put them in moss, for this goes sour.

Brandlings A good bait especially for bream, tench, and perch. They are small, red worms found in manure and compost heaps and kept in this they will remain alive for weeks, but they must not be exposed to the sun.

Mussels A bait readily accepted by most fish. Can be used in part or whole, the hook size depending upon the size of mussel. For a whole one, use a No. 6, passed through the yellow part.

Wheat A very fine bait indeed, especially during the six or seven weeks following harvest time, It is most useful in waters where minnows abound, when paste, maggots, etc., are almost useless. Care must be taken when ground-baiting, for wheat sinks quickly, reaching bottom almost where it was thrown in. Also, it being solid stuff, one can quickly overfeed the fish. For a given swim a quarter as much of wheat as you would use of maggots is about right.

One grain on a No. 12 hook or, for big fish, two grains on a No. 10, is satisfactory.

Wheat must be boiled to the correct consistency – this is very important. The best method is to soak it in cold water for twenty-four hours; then bring it to the boil, turn down the heat, and stew as slowly as possible until the grains are split open, well swollen, and soft. This may require a little practice at first, but to obtain the best results it must be right.

Sweetcorn This bait has become very popular, especially for tench and bream. Just buy a small tin.

Sausage meat This is now an established bait. Care should be taken when mixing, however, for used alone it is much too tacky. Get some breadcrumbs (or sausage rusk); mix into a paste, then add the sausage meat until it is nice and soft. This is an excellent bait for most species, barbel in particular.

Finally, don't be tempted to put oils, such as aniseed, into your bait; you won't catch any more fish. There is no secret formula for bait; if yours is properly mixed, and correctly presented, you have nothing to worry about.

Crayfish The crayfish is a freshwater lobster, up to about 5 inches long, which is found under stones and in holes in the banks. It is dark green in colour and an excellent bait for chub and possibly barbel. Pass the hook, a No. 2, through its tail from the underside, leaving the point and barb showing. Best fished on a leger, and after casting, jerked back towards you on the bottom. Failing this, it can be legered stationary. A small one, about 2–3 inches in length, is best.

Baiting with crayfish

Live baiting This means using a live fish as a bait to catch larger predators such as pike and perch. It is becoming increasingly frowned upon, and is banned on some waters.

5 Legering

Legering is a form of fishing where no float is used; an extremely deadly method, especially when you are seeking specimen fish. It is not new by any means, but only a few years ago it was considered to be rather crude, with its heavy lead, stout line and rod, and the passive angler, waiting for the rod to be pulled into the water. However, more and more anglers nowadays are legering properly, sitting intently watching the rod top or line, and catching good fish. It is a fascinating method indeed, though not a magical one. Only a foolish angler always legers, but used in the right place, at the right time, it is a very good method.

Many anglers when legering experience difficulty in knowing when to strike (see also page 23). The rod top may jerk forward quickly an inch or so, or frequently the rod top will pull round several inches. Sometimes when fishing fast water the rod top will be bent over by the pressure of the water on the line, then suddenly it will jerk backwards; this may be a bite, it may not. However, most bites which make the rod top move quickly are difficult to strike.

The solution is that your tackle must be such that a bite results in the rod top moving slowly whether it moves backwards or forwards. When a fish picks up the bait it should move off slowly, even if only for an inch or two; consequently, the rod top follows equally slowly. Whatever type of bite you get, providing the rod top moves slowly, you should hook the fish. Many things contribute to this; the rod, line, and water speed to mention just three; but the most important to my mind is the set-up of the terminal tackle or trace.

The most common method is to have a drilled bullet (a circular-shaped lead with a hole through) running up and down the line stopped by a shot the required distance from the hook. There is, however, a much better method: the 'sliding link', and this is how it works.

The sliding link

TO ROD
TO LEAD
TO HOOK

The sliding link Attach a length of nylon 6 inches long to one $\frac{1}{8}$-inch-diameter split ring, tying a knot in the nylon an inch from the end. Pinch a swan shot on to the nylon; this is called the

Above: legering in fast-flowing water, the rod well up, bottom of handle tucked into groin and line over finger

Legering in slow or medium-fast water, the rod is dipped, handle tucked under the arm, helping to keep the rod still

'link'. After threading the line through the rod rings take the 'link' and pass the line through the split ring. Now pinch a small split shot on the line 12 inches or so from the end to prevent the 'link' from slipping off and finally attach the hook. The 'link' will now slide up and down the line and all is ready.

When a fish picks up your bait it pulls the line through the split ring and not through a drilled bullet. This results in a much slower bite, and one which is easier to hook. Since using this rig, my catches have doubled, and it is now widely used in most parts of the country.

If you cannot obtain small rings another method is to fold a length of nylon and tie the two ends together; then attach the shots. Although satisfactory, it isn't quite as effective as the split ring especially when the fish are biting shyly.

Another advantage with this rig is the ease with which you can add or take off lead as required. If you discover that additional swan shots are necessary to hold, or roll, bottom; right then extra shot is added. Or if you find that you have too many shots on the link it is a simple matter to remove one or two as desired.

In a matter of seconds you can adjust your weight exactly, whereas with a bullet or similar lead attached direct to the line it means dismantling your tackle, which can be a nuisance, especially in cold or wet weather.

Arlesey bomb on line

The Arlesey bomb I do not always use a 'sliding link', however, especially with a heavy weight ($\frac{1}{2}$ oz. or over). In these circumstances I like the Arlesey Bomb, which is an extremely good lead. The line passes through the swivel in the top, and the lead is prevented from slipping down on the hook by a split shot.

The strike When a fish takes the bait and has it properly in its mouth the strike is made which drives the hook into the fish. The strike is best explained by saying it consists of an upward, fairly quick motion of the rod. In some circumstances – when fishing under trees, for example – the strike is made sideways to prevent the rod hitting overhanging branches, etc. At no time should the strike be powerful, otherwise the line may break.

When to strike
As for when to strike, my rule, broadly speaking, is this. Watch for the slightest movement on the rod top or line, and strike at anything that moves slowly, however slight. The rod top may move only $\frac{1}{2}$ inch, or it may move 6 inches, and I strike at these movements, except when using worms and sometimes also paste as a bait, when I wait for a second pull.

I have described the different bites to expect in the 'fish' chapters, and this advice, coupled with that already given, i.e. striking at any slow movement, should result in your catching plenty of fish. As you gain experience, you will begin to recognize the different bites and know almost intuitively which to strike at.

Always, if possible, hold the rod. This is not easy, I know but very few anglers can pick a rod up from a rod-rest correctly and strike at the same time. If you must use a rest, use two, one supporting the rod at the ferrule, and one under the handle. Keep your hands close to the rod handle, ready for instant action. By holding the rod, how-ever, you can have the line over one finger, and often, you will feel the bite but not see it on the rod tip, especially in a wind. Hold the rod low, if possible, with the top nearly touching the water; in this way you can hold it steady and also it doesn't catch the wind. An exception to this is when fishing fast water, when the rod should be held high, other-wise water pressure on the line will pull the bait away from the desired spot.

Holding the rod while legering so that it can be kept perfectly still

Above all, concentrate. Don't gaze about, but keep your eyes glued on the rod top. Many bites are feeble ones difficult to see, but these are often the biggest fish. Keep your mind on the job.

Bite-indicators
In recent years, both swing-tips and quiver-tips have become popular and I prefer the latter. This consists of a thin, tapered length of fibre-glass attached to the rod top, which makes bite detection easier. At first, however, I suggest you hold the rod and watch the rod top with your finger on the line; this way you are in direct contact with the fish. Should you wish to try a quiver-tip, then do so. Here, the rod can be held but with a rod rest supporting the rod about halfway down the top joint.

Fishing at dawn on a misty morning

6 On catching big fish

Every angler dreams of catching big fish, but there are very many anglers who go through life catching small or medium-sized ones; very occasionally a big one comes their way, usually by accident. This is called 'a fish of a lifetime', but with the correct approach, big fish will come your way quite often.

To catch a big fish, however, you must approach your fishing with a different attitude from that of the majority of anglers. You must be prepared to experience many blank days; you will use baits that are intended to stop the small fish biting, with tackle that, should a big fish be hooked, is capable of landing it.

Richard Walker in his book *Still Water Angling* lists five main essentials for the catching of specimen fish. They are as follows: (1) you must first locate the fish; (2) having done that you must not frighten it away; (3) you must use suitable tackle; (4) then choose the right time to fish, and finally (5) you must then use the right bait.

Later in this book, in the 'fish' chapters, I shall tell you how to locate your fish. There are, of course, many other ways than the ones I have recommended, but these you will learn with experience.

Having found your fish, get into a position where you do not frighten it. This may entail crawling about on hands and knees (and often on your stomach). If you clump about on the skyline, and bang a box or basket down on the bank, you won't catch many big fish.

Make sure your tackle is sound. Do not use inferior tackle, and if you think the line is rotten buy a new one, or you will regret it. Choosing the right time to fish is very important. Remember you must be there when the fish are feeding. They won't wait for you to come! If you think you stand a chance at night, then fish at night, and in the summer don't lie in bed waiting for the breakfast to be brought up. Usually during the summer months you arrive home in time for breakfast. Take different types of bait, and always carry worms and bread. Don't be afraid to use a natural bait, such as crayfish. Give the fish what they want, not what you think they should have.

Specimen hunting often entails fishing one swim for several hours at a time. Your bait may not be in the right spot, or it may not be presented in the correct manner. Unless you are convinced that both method and bait are right you must experiment, and the angler in his early days of specimen hunting may find this trying. After legering, say a lump of cheese for a couple of hours without a bite, it takes persistence to change to a worm for a further two hours. But that is specimen hunting.

The more the merrier

Your fishing will be more enjoyable (and productive) if you are part of a group. Specimen-hunters' clubs have become popular and members fish together in twos and threes. All knowledge gained is shared by all, so if someone locates a swim holding big fish, he tells the others, the idea being that it does not matter who catches the fish so long as someone does.

A common question is: 'Does noise frighten fish?' There is noise and noise. It has been proved beyond doubt that you can shout or even sing and it does not affect the fishing in the slightest. Fish are not scared by such noises. What does scare them are vibrations, such as stamping or thumping a box or basket down upon the bank. Anything that shakes the ground must be avoided at all costs.

However, I regularly fish a lake in which we catch many tench, and a railway runs alongside it. Every few minutes a train rumbles past, and the ground really shudders, but the fish are not frightened, because this is a vibration that they have grown used to. Even in this particular lake, though, a heavy footstep is enough to put the tench away.

7 Roach

For most anglers, the roach is the most popular freshwater fish as well as the commonest.

The body is, more or less, elliptical in shape and in some waters is deep-bellied while in others it is slim. The colouration of the back varies, depending largely upon the water, but a dark green is common. The flanks also vary, but are generally silvery with intermediate colouring between. The fins, generally speaking, are orange and red, with a greyish dorsal fin. It is not in the prime of condition until November, being covered with slime during the summer months.

There cannot be an angler who has never caught one. For most people it is their main quarry, and it takes great skill to catch big bags consistently in all conditions. To catch a two-pounder is the ambition of most anglers, but I always consider a one-pounder worthy of capture.

It is generally accepted that early morning and late evening fishing is essential in summer. While I prefer to fish at these hours, it is by no means essential, and I have taken many big bags of good-quality fish when the sun has been scorching my back. It is important, however, to fish in the right place during the heat of the day.

In summer always fish where there is most oxygen in the water, weir-pools and weed-beds being two such places. Weeds give out oxygen by day, and carbon dioxide at night, and when you are fishing in the middle of the day your bait should be in the vicinity of weed-beds, and very often *in* them. When I am seeking roach in summer, immediately the sun becomes hot I walk along the bank until I find a 'cabbage patch'. 'Cabbages' (lilies of which the tops do not reach the surface of the water) appear from the bank to be dark brown, though they are really green. They are inhabited by most species of fish and are the finest places for catching roach; it is a poor day indeed when they fail to produce any. 'Onions' – that is bulrushes with a small brown flower on top, growing in gravel – are my second choice and should always be given a try. There are, of course, many other types of weed that hold roach, but in my experience, these are the most profitable.

Weir-pools are extremely good places in summer. The difficulty lies in finding a clear area of bottom on which to fish, since they are often full of boulders and snags. Keep trying until you find a clear bottom – it need only be a yard square – and get your bait on it. A good place to try is at the 'tail' where the deep water joins the shallows. As the evening approaches, get out of the pool and fish the shallows just below. There may not be a fish on them during the day but with the approach of evening they drop back to them, feeding madly.

The weed-beds where you caught fish while the sun was up will not fish well towards dark, but by fishing a few yards away from them in the 'open' water, your sport should continue.

At the beginning of November conditions change, and from then to March the fish are in the prime of condition. Try swims where 'cabbages' grew in summer, for the roach love to ferret among the old roots. The 'onions' will have died off now, taking the colour of dark brown, the tops in many cases being barely visible above the surface. The speed of water is broken up by these rushes, and a bait cast into the slack water just behind them is usually taken.

Many writers advise fishing the eddies in winter, and while this is sometimes successful – especially during very cold weather – I prefer to fish the fast or fairly fast water. Roach like a little stream, providing the water is not too cold, and will generally be found in the straight, fast reaches running over a gravel bottom. The water may *look* fast, but it is not so fast on the bottom, where the bait will be.

Tackle THE ROD: 11 feet fibre-glass with full stand-off rings.
THE LINE: I use a 5 lb. b.s. for legering and a 4 lb. b.s. for 'trotting'. A finer one, say 2 lb. b.s., will be advisable for canals, especially in clear water.

THE REEL: a fixed-spool, or a centre-pin for canal fishing.
TERMINAL TACKLE: When legering, use the 'sliding link'
method as described in the legering chapter. For float
fishing the split shots are pinched on the line in a bunch,
and the hook tied direct.

Roach can be taken by a variety of methods, float
legering, 'trotting-down' (page 31), 'stret pegging' (page 32)
and legering, the method depending upon the time of the
year and the water being fished. Experience has taught me
that on rivers with little or no stream, in summer there is
no finer method than legering, and I have taken big bags
with it when others have failed.

Legering   The amount of 'trail', that is, the distance of line between
lead and bait, is important, the length of this depending
upon the swim being fished. If I am fishing 'cabbages' I like
a short one of 6 inches, and the same when I am fishing
'onions'. When little stream is running, I find that bites are
more easily detected by the use of a short 'trail'. The lead
consists of one or two swan shots, depending upon conditions. Always remember that the sooner you can tighten up
your bait, the sooner a bite will be detected.

If you are fishing 'cabbages', seat yourself in a position
at the top of the patch, and throw in a couple of handfuls
of ground-bait on top of the end 'cabbage'. Ground-bait is
used for attracting fish to a swim and holding them there.
For this purpose, soaked breadcrumbs are best. Cast over
and beyond the end 'cabbage', and when the bait hits
bottom, wind in quickly until the bait is *under* the 'cabbage'

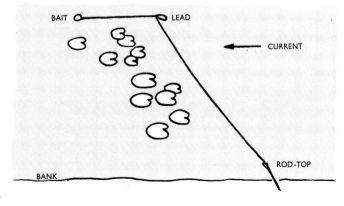

Legering in 'cabbages'

You should not have very long to wait. Be prepared for a bite the moment you stop winding.

Bites will vary. The tip may move forward slowly – anything from $\frac{1}{2}$ an inch to 6 inches : it may move backwards; or it may jerk forward an inch, jerking forward a further 2 inches almost immediately. These are the usual run of bites, although you will get others. I cannot tell you when you strike – this only comes with experience – but if you strike at anything that moves you will not go far wrong. Do not wait for second pulls if the tip moves slowly, however slightly, but strike *at once*. If bites are not forthcoming, after a few minutes move the bait a fraction, for something may be covering it up. This results in a bite nine times out of ten. When you hook a roach under the 'cabbages' it usually requires plenty of 'bullying' to get it out, hence my 5 lb b.s. line. I often see a 'cabbage' floating down river after I have landed a fish!

Tactics are more or less the same when legering away from weeds, but it is essential to keep the bait moving. Cast just beyond the spot where the ground-bait has landed and every two minutes or so wind in a little line. Keep this up until the bait is well on your side of the ground-bait and then recast, this time slightly lower downstream. Bites will come at any time, usually when you move the bait, and the rod should be kept very still while doing this. If you find this difficult, gently pull the rod to one side. Be careful that you do not eventually pull it back too far, otherwise the rod will be in a position which makes it difficult to strike properly.

The same applies when legering close to 'onions'. Place the ground-bait so that it trickles through them *just* on the outside, and your bait so that it comes to rest as close to the outside rushes as possible. Accurate casting is essential; cast downstream and wind the bait back into position.

Fishing with silkweed

Another effective method of catching roach in summer is to fish a piece of silkweed down the fast water of a weir. (First of all make sure you are allowed to fish from the weir.) Silkweed is the green weed which grows on the weir, which in many cases will be very thick, one's feet sinking into it. It is attached to the hook by casting over and dragging the hook through it. The float is then set about

12 inches from the bait and allowed to drop into the water just over the 'sill'. Allow it to travel down just outside the fast water until the end of the pool is reached. Bites will occur at any time and are definite, the float either going under or sideways. Some anglers insist that the weed must not be touched by hand, and from experience I must agree.

Trotting down

'Trotting down' is a form of float fishing whereby the float and bait are allowed to travel down with the current, the bait being fished any distance off the bottom depending upon the species, time of year, etc. When September comes the river changes, the leaves are falling, and a little stream is running. At this time of year legering 'goes off', for several reasons. The fish, I am convinced, expect to see a moving bait, one off the bottom, and will not turn over a lot of dead leaves in order to find their food. 'Trotting down' is by far the best method for the next two months.

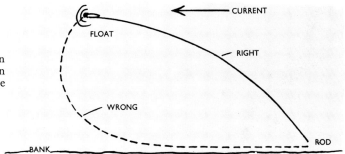

Controlling the line when 'trotting down', as seen from above

The amount of ground-bait used is important. For wide rivers, a great quantity is advisable, say a canvas bucketful for four hours' fishing. Maggots can either be mixed into the ground-bait or thrown in loose; for rivers such as the Thames I prefer the former method; on the small streams the latter. I rarely find bread in any form necessary as ground-bait on the little rivers, a large quantity of maggots being sufficient. When fishing the wide rivers three or four handfuls of ground-bait should be thrown in slightly up-stream of where you intend fishing and usually in the middle of the river, for the fish are found as a rule where there is most current. Bait up with three or four maggots and after adjusting the float to the correct depth, cast to the desired spot. An overhead cast will be the best for long, accurate casting. The bait should travel downstream, the lead just tripping the bottom. Line control is important. Avoid a big 'bow', for this causes drag, and it is most important that the bait travels down naturally. Constant flicking back of the line is necessary in order to keep it tight, and you are constantly on the go. It is hard work.

Bites will vary, but are, as a rule, definite. The float may go straight under; travel across stream; dip slightly and carry on faster than it should; or it may lift in the water. Whatever bite you get, strike immediately, pulling the rod back over your shoulder. This may appear rather vicious striking, but with perhaps 20 yards of line to pick up, it is necessary. If you fail to get bites, or if, after a while, they stop, experiment. Moving the float an inch or two up or down can make all the difference, and the fish are often taken at mid-water. Keep trying different depths all the time. Regular ground-baiting must be kept up while catching fish, say a couple of handfuls at a time. Remember, you may have a big shoal of roach in the swim and they must be kept interested. They will soon move if they are not.

When fishing narrow rivers, tactics are more or less the same. In many cases floats and weights need not be so heavy, and there is no need for long casting.

Stret-pegging With November, 'stret-pegging' comes into its own. This is a form of float fishing in which the bait is fished on the bottom, with the line taut between rod top and float. Paste, crust, and maggots are all good baits, but the last-named are my favourite. Having chosen your swim, introduce a little ground-bait, making sure that it comes to rest *exactly*

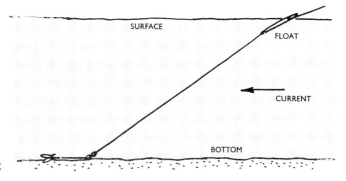

Stret-pegging

where your bait will lie. If, say, the depth is 5 feet, push the float up 6 feet from the bait. Cast, making sure that the line is tight between rod top and float, and allow the bait to roll round until it comes to rest where the ground-bait has been introduced.

Make sure – and this is important – that the bait rolls in a natural manner, always keeping the line tight. Watch carefully for the bites. The float may move slightly out towards midstream, dipping as it does so; it may slide gently under; or a sharp pluck may occur. These are the most likely bites, but watch for everything and strike at once. Sometimes, however, I have begun to miss fish, and if this occurs give them a second or two longer. Take some coloured maggots, red and yellow ones especially. Often the fish seem to prefer these to white.

Ground-bait should be used sparingly. Use lumps the size of a pigeon's egg, and introduce them at about fifteen-minute intervals. If I am fishing with maggots in smaller streams, I use them also as ground-bait; breadcrumbs cannot be bettered as ground-bait.

Fishing in very cold weather

Fishing is often difficult during periods of extreme cold or immediately after a frost; the roach are disinclined to feed, lying lethargic on the bottom. On such days fish the slack water, and adjust the float so that an inch only protrudes above the surface, and the lead, one or two swan shots, *just* touches bottom. Go easy with the ground-bait. Use a piece the size of a walnut to start with, and repeat at intervals. Failing this, a few maggots (if being used on the hook) will be enough.

Do not be in a hurry to strike when you get a bite; let the float go well away. The fish, on picking up the bait, will hold it just between its lips, often for some time, before deciding to eat it. If using one maggot, use a No. 16 hook; but with two maggots, change to a No. 14. Breadcrust is also good on such days, but keep the pieces small, about $\frac{1}{4}$ inch square.

This procedure, of course, may vary from water to water. On some, half an inch of float showing may be ample, especially in calm conditions. Also a float carrying no more than one swan shot may be sufficient. Always experiment if bites are not forthcoming.

Fishing canals Canals require much understanding. It is important that the bait is in the right spot of course, and this is rarely in the middle of the canal, although the water is usually deepest here. It is on the slopes on either side of the channel, that the fish generally feed, not in the centre. During summer, silkweed (or blanket-weed as it is often called) makes bottom fishing difficult, and the roach are taken either on a slowly sinking bait, or one that rests on top of the silkweed. As a sinking bait maggots are best, one on a No. 16 hook, or two on a No. 14 being sufficient. Choose a float that carries one shot and nip this on the line 18 inches from the hook. A handful of 'cloud' ground-bait is thrown in before fishing, followed by a few maggots from time to time. Cloud ground-bait is mixed so lightly that upon entering the water it breaks up into a 'cloud' and does not sink quickly to the bottom. Only have the tip of the float showing, and strike at the first movement. You may say to yourself, 'That can't be a bite', but it often is; and if in any doubt, strike. Once the bait has reached bottom, retrieve and re-cast, and inspect the maggots each time. Always rebait with fresh ones each time you catch a fish.

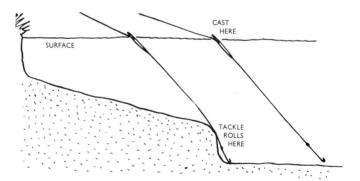

Fishing on the slope
of a canal

If you decide that bait fished on top of the silkweed will produce results, then breadcrust takes some beating. Pinch the shot on the line 4 inches above a No. 12 or No. 14 hook.

Canals fish well in winter. At this time of year I like my bait on the bottom, especially if I am seeking good fish. Maggots and bread are acceptable, but you must experiment until you find the right bait. For baits other than crust, place the shot 12 inches above the hook; for crust, begin with the shot 2 inches away, but alter this distance if bites are not forthcoming or are difficult to strike. Cast into the middle of the canal, and allow the bait to roll round on to the slope, and hold it there. Don't strike at the first indication, but wait until the float moves off or goes under.

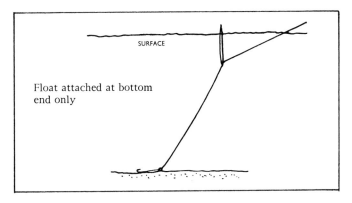

SURFACE

Float attached at bottom end only

If an upstream wind is blowing, the float is best attached by the bottom only, and the strike is a sideways one, with the rod tip nearly touching the water. In calm conditions the float can be attached top and bottom if you prefer, but don't have too much line on the water.

A 6 lb 6 oz chub
taken by the author

8 Chub

Description and location

A lesson in concealment. Ian Tolputt has hidden himself well enough to deceive even a chub

The chub is similar in shape to the roach but more 'solid'. Its mouth is a large one, and the tail, unlike that of the roach, black. Its anal fin is convex, where on the roach and dace it is concave. Chub are often confused with roach, and especially dace, but there is no need for such confusion. Apart from the anal fin, it is a far more sturdy, powerful fish, with big leathery lips, and is a most popular quarry. The chub ranks high on my own list; he is not fussy when it comes to food, and possesses cunning second to none. The angler who can consistently stalk chub without scaring them, need have no fears about his camouflage and silent approach.

The chub is not in condition until the end of summer – but a three-pounder hooked on light tackle in a weir-pool will give a fair scrap. Try the fast water and the shallows at the 'tail', or the shallows at evening. In the open river chub will be found under the willow trees or alongside 'onions', cruising a few inches below the surface, and, in the small streams especially, among the 'cabbages'. The whole of the fish may not be visible, perhaps only the big black tail, and extreme caution is necessary to catch them. Gaps between 'onions' through which the stream passes should also be watched, for the chub will sooner or later swim into them.

Chub love overhead cover, where, for instance, a branch has fallen into the water, gathering the rubbish as it floats downstream. This is my favourite type of chub swim; a bait, correctly presented under, or close to it, rarely fails.

With the approach of winter, chub fishing really starts. The most likely places are old 'onion-beds', where trees overhang, or have fallen into the water, alongside clay banks, or on the bend of a river where the current is suddenly diverted. Don't be afraid to fish the middle of the river, providing it is not too fast, especially in the wider rivers.

These are the usual types of chub swims, but the greatest thing an angler can possess is the ability to 'read' the water, looking at the swim and visualising what it contains. This comes with experience, of course. If a swim looks 'chubby', fish it.

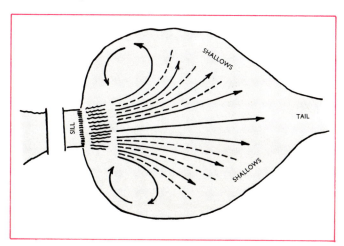

A typical weir-pool. Arrows show current; dotted lines are likely tracks for float tackle

Tackle   THE ROD : As for bream and roach.

THE LINE : For legering, 6 lb. b.s. For float fishing and floating crust, 4 lb. b.s.

THE REEL : Fixed-spool.

TERMINAL TACKLE : When legering, use either the 'sliding link' or Arlesey Bomb, direct to line. For float fishing, a shot, or shots pinched on the line, with hook tied direct.

Fishing under an overhanging willow

Float fishing in summer

Chub can be caught throughout the season on a wide variety of baits and methods. In summer, float fishing will account for many fish even when the sun is high in the sky, two good baits being bread and minnows.

During the first few weeks of the season good sport will be had in and around the weir pools using minnows as bait. Get a small piece of cork about an inch across, and bore a hole through it. Push the line through this, and then ram a piece of stick in the hole, to hold it in position. Pinch on a swan shot 12 inches from a No. 8 hook. Plug the cork so that it is about 3 feet from the live minnow, hooked through the top lip only.

Begin by casting into the fast water, and allow the bait to travel down with the current, until either you get a bite, or it reaches the shallows. If no bites are forthcoming, cast in a different spot, allowing the bait to search as much of the pool as possible. A bite is signalled by the cork suddenly disappearing from view, or, if it is on the shallows, travelling across stream sideways. In either case the strike should be instantaneous.

Another good method is 'trotting', using either crust or flake. A float should be used which carries enough shot to ensure that the bait reaches bottom quickly : two, three, or four swan shots are usually right. Set the float so that the bait is about 2 feet off bottom, and bunch the shots about 15 inches from the hook. A No. 6 is about right. Allow the float to pass naturally through the swim, and strike immediately the float signals a bite. This is indicated by the float either disappearing rapidly, or suddenly 'lifting' in the water, or falling over at half-cock, or travelling downstream faster than it should. Make sure the line floats, and that not too much slack is on the water.

Floating crust This is a most enjoyable method and an extremely deadly one. On the line tie a No. 6 hook – nothing else. Get a new loaf and break off a piece of crust about 2 inches square and place this on the hook. Cast upstream of a likely-looking spot and allow the crust to float down on the surface making sure the line is straight and not bowed, otherwise, the crust will be pulled along and the chub will not take it. When the crust disappears – either in a swirl, or sucked under – wait for two or three seconds and strike. You won't hook every fish but you should catch more than you miss. One important point: before you cast, drop the crust in the water for a second; this will give it extra weight and make casting easier.

Legering in summer My favourite method at this time of year is to fish a large lump of cheese-paste on a No. 6 hook, casting at individual fish. You spot a chub, which is usually on or just below the surface, and by creeping and crawling you approach within casting distance. Great caution is necessary. One false move, and the chub will disappear. If the stream is a shallow one, look among the streamer weed, for the chub lie under those long, trailing masses, moving out occasionally to intercept passing food.

Having got into position with the cheese on the hook (nothing else is on the line, not even a weight), cast so that the bait lands some 2 or 3 feet in front of the chub, and a little to one side. Watch the bait, and if the chub takes it, give him a second to close his mouth, then strike. If the bait is refused, recast, so that it lands just behind the chub with a plop; often the fish will whip round and take it.

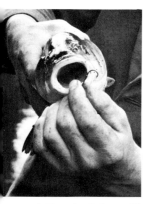

A No. 2 hook is not big when placed alongside the mouth of a 3-lb. chub

If a chub can be seen in the streamer weed, cast the bait *into* the weed several feet in front of the fish. Work the bait through the weed and be prepared for the chub to accept it *after* it has passed him. He will often watch it go past, turn round, and chase it downstream.

Peter Drennan took this 4½-lb chub on bread-flake

Legering in winter in small rivers

These small rivers, I find, often require a different technique from the bigger ones. Many of them are very overgrown in summer, and if 'onions' predominate, only their tops will now be visible. The chub lie up by these weeds, and I like my bait somewhere near them. The fish do, of course, move into the weed-free areas, especially on mild days, when they are more inclined to roam, so try these places if bites are not forthcoming in the weedy swims.

Usually, in these rivers, 'rolling the bottom' is almost impossible, owing to the weeds. The bait is therefore anchored in one particular spot, and if a chub fails to pick it up within fifteen minutes, move on. Choose a lead that will just hold bottom, cast into the required spot and hold it there. If you use cheese-paste, one or two samples of this thrown in well ahead of the swim will do for groundbait. There is no need for large handfuls of breadcrumbs in these small rivers.

Both cheese-paste and breadcrust should be tried. If the day is fairly mild, pieces about 1½ ins square on a No. 6 hook should be used, but on cold days when the chub tend to move about less, pieces ¾ inch square on a No. 10 will give you a better chance of success. When using big pieces of crust, the amount of lead must be increased, in order to keep the crust down. Crust is extremely buoyant, and a piece match-box size, will lift a $\frac{1}{4}$ oz. weight off the bottom.

When fishing crust the lead is stopped with a shot 2 inches from the hook. Mashed bread is best for ground bait, but don't use too much. Bites will be as described earlier, even with big pieces of crust, and the bite is often a feeble one, so look out!

Legering in winter in wide rivers

When November comes, chub fishing really starts. Breadcrust, flake, lobs, and cheese-paste are the best baits, the last being my favourite. Taking it all round, cheese-paste is an extremely fine chub bait, and it is a poor day when it is refused.

Select your swim and experiment with different weights until you have it so that it will roll the bottom. The rod top will tell you this. It will pull over an inch or two, remaining in that position for twenty seconds or so, then, as the current moves the lead the rod top will jerk backwards almost immediately pulling over again. Should the

The author returns a 4¾-lb chub taken on breadcrust

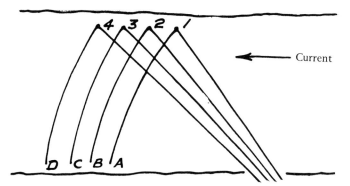

Rolling the leger. Cast
to 1, 2, 3, 4, in succession.
Current swings tackle to
A, B, C, D.

top remain pulled over for too long the lead is too heavy :
if it doesn't pull over but continues jerking then the lead
is too light. See where it finally comes to rest. If you decide
that this is where the chub should be, throw in a couple of
handfuls of ground-bait. This must be heavy so that it
reaches bottom quickly, but breaks up on doing so. Bait
with a big piece of cheese-paste on a No. 4 hook, which
should be about 15 inches from the lead. Cast well out,
across and downstream, wait until the line tightens, and
watch the rod top. On hitting bottom, the lead should, if
of the correct weight, remain stationary for a few minutes,
and then roll a few inches, before stopping again. Keep this
up until it has passed through the line of ground-bait, and is
resting near your bank. Then recast, slightly lower downstream until you get a bite.

Now for the bite. The rod top may move forward slowly
some 3 inches; it may jerk back sharply, remaining in that
position; it may move backwards and forwards half an
inch at a time, or it may give a short, sharp jerk. Whatever
happens, strike *at once*, and you will rarely miss. You will,
of course, get many variation of bites, but generally speaking, strike at the first knock or pull.

If you catch a chub, throw in a little more ground-bait,
say one good handful, but in any case, do not go too long
without additional ground-bait. Keep the fish interested.

Legering upstream in small streams in winter

I am now thinking of those little streams that are
reasonably free of weed, but have a nice bit of cover, such
as overhanging trees. Usually we leger downstream, but
upstream legering is also a very effective method.

Having decided upon your swim, tackle up with one

swan shot pinched on the line 12 inches above a No. 6 hook. By creeping or crawling, you approach the spot, and having carefully done this, crouch down just below it. Cast upstream ahead of the swim, quickly take up any slack line, and gather it in as the bait – either crust, cheese, paste, or flake – travels downstream towards you. Bites will occur at any time, and do not expect any 'clouts'. If a bite is felt, it will be a very slight one, or the line may tighten slightly, or may travel downstream faster than it ought. At any of these indications, strike at once.

If a bite has not occurred when the bait is opposite you, allow it to continue downstream until the current forces it off the bottom. When the bait is opposite or downstream of you, a bite is generally felt, consisting of a sharp pluck on the line. Wait about two seconds after feeling this and then strike. You can't miss!

Remember, strike at *anything* suspicious; you often get a surprise. Do not expect to catch several chub in the same swim, and it pays to keep moving about.

The author checks the weight of a 4¼-lb chub

These chub were taken from the River Evenlode – on a very cold day!

Do not watch the rod top, but the line, at the point where it enters the water, and *always* hold it between your fingers. One bite you may see, the next you may only feel, but providing you are concentrating, you will not miss many fish.

Float fishing in winter

Chub can be taken by long-trotting, or 'swimming the stream', but another effective method is to fish the slack water when the day is extremely cold. In 1963 I arrived at the river to find it completely covered with ice, but succeeded in breaking a small hole. I scattered a few maggots into the hole, and placed two of these on a No. 16 hook. The float carried one B.B. shot. I fished with the bait *just* on bottom, and the bites consisted of a tiny ring appearing round the float, nothing more. I caught several chub up to 3 lb. that day, but for this method the water must be completely slack.

9 Tench

Description and location

The tench is found more in still waters than in rivers. Like the chub, it is a big, stocky, powerful fish, with enormous fins and tail. The eyes are similar to those of an eel, small and red, and the fish vary in colour from black to an orange-yellow, depending upon the water. I fish one lake where they are jet black, and yet in a nearby gravel-pit they are a beautiful yellow, apart from their backs, which are green.

Tench are primarily a summer fish, although they are taken in winter during mild weather, or floodwater. Usually they provide relaxing fishing, when one sits back, awaiting that familiar slide-away of the float.

Tench love lilies, blanket-weed, and mud – 'Deep, black, smelly mud,' as Fred Taylor once wrote. Even so, they will not *always* feed in such swims, and the time of year and day also enter into it. Generally speaking, tench appear to follow a set pattern. In the early weeks of the season they are found in the shallower water of the lake and they retire to the deeps about mid-summer. With the approach of autumn they move back to the shallows for the winter.

Many writers advise facing the wind in still waters, but Fred Taylor suggests that this does not always apply to shallow waters, and my own experience bears this out. It can, however, be a decided advantage in a deep lake or reservoir, and this should be remembered.

A 5¼-lb. tench taken by Fred Towns on float tackle in a gravel pit

The easiest way of locating tench is to watch for the tell-tale bubbles they send up when feeding. Tench bubbles are small and frothy, and appear in large numbers. They are often accompanied by small pieces of stick, rush, etc., thrown up by the tench. Always fish swims where this occurs. Tench also 'roll' on the surface as do bream, and when you see this happen, fish there.

Although tench are associated with warm weather, I don't fish exclusively on those beautiful evenings which we often read about, when the lake is still, and the sun setting. I take many good bags on rough, blowy days, providing the wind is not a cold one, and also in light rain.

Tench are not usually fished for during winter, but will feed in rivers when in flood. Heavy water appears to wake them from their wintry stupor, and in these conditions good fish are often taken.

Tackle

THE ROD : As for roach.

THE LINE : 5 lb. b.s. (6 lb. in very weedy waters).

THE REEL : Fixed-spool.

TERMINAL TACKLE : For float fishing, a shot or shots pinched on the line. When legering, use the 'sliding link'.

Ground-baiting

Ground-baiting is important. It is done in several ways, depending on whether you choose the swim in the morning or evening, or bait up the swim several days before fishing. Pre-baiting is discussed at the end of this chapter. If you choose your swim on arrival and want to fish immediately, I should drag the swim, in preference to ground-baiting. This is what I do under these circumstances. Tench are attracted to a swim that has just been dragged, which has the effect of stirring up the bottom, thereby releasing food, and colouring the water. My drag is a simple affair consisting of two garden-rake heads bolted together, attached to a length of strong rope. Pull the drag through the swim a dozen times, and finish off by introducing a few samples of the hook-bait.

Double-sided rake

Float fishing

When fishing stillwaters the float is attached by the bottom only. The line is thus sunk below the surface, which prevents the float and bait from blowing about. Find the depth of the swim, adjust the float so that the bait is just, and *only just* on bottom, the lead being 12 inches from the hook. When using crust, however, I like it much closer, about 4 inches.

Bites generally follow the same pattern. The float will rise slightly in the water, or dip a little, and then move to one side, gradually sinking out of sight. Wait until it is almost under before striking. If you fail to hook the tench, the next time delay the strike until the float has completely disappeared. Use a fairly big hook; I like a No. 8 unless using maggots, when I go down to a No. 12 or 14. Because the float is attached by the bottom only, the strike must be a sideways one.

Often tench do not bite in this manner, and I have found this especially so in rough conditions. I first experienced it in Ireland, when during the course of an evening, I had several bites that resulted in the float dipping sharply, nothing else. I suspected roach, but after a while decided to experiment. I held the rod, and struck when the float dipped. The result: a tench. I had many good tench that week, and also in the following year, when the bites were generally the same. When tench are biting in this manner I hold the rod, but usually, when waiting for the float to sink away, this is not necessary.

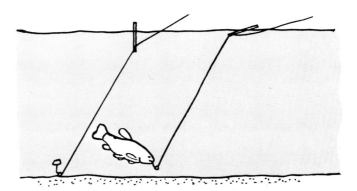

The 'lift' method

The 'lift' method A few years ago the Taylor brothers publicized the following method by which once again the fish is struck immediately the float moves. The float is a length of peacock quill attached by the bottom only, and the shot placed about *an inch* from the hook. This method is used when the

A 7½-lb tench is returned

tench, although feeding, are interested in small baits only, but it does not follow that catching them is easy. The bait is often picked up, and spat out again immediately; a fast strike is therefore necessary. Crust is the best bait, small pieces about $\frac{1}{2}$ inch square on a No. 12 or No. 14 hook being just right.

Set the float so that you are fishing about 4 inches deeper than the actual depth; cast, and draw the tackle tight. A rod-rest is essential, for you cannot hold the rod. Bites are registered by the float lifting and falling flat, and the strike – a sideways one – is instantaneous. While this is a deadly method, there are some waters where it fails.

Legering in gravel pits

Fishing for tench in gravel pits has become very popular during the last decade and one very effective method is legering maggots in conjunction with a blockend feeder. The most popular feeders are Peter Drennan's Feederlinks which are available in three sizes; the smallest takes 15-20 maggots, the middle size 30-40 and the largest 90-100. The feeder is stopped by a leger stop between 12-15 ins from the hook which is baited with maggots. For two maggots use a No. 16

A tench comes to net

hook, for three or four, a No. 14 or 12. For most occasions the middle-size feeder is best. The feeders are sold with two swan shots attached to the link which should be sufficient for casts of up to 30 yards.

An important point is the sequence in which the baiting of the hook and filling of the feeder is done. ALWAYS bait the hook first, then fill the feeder: fill the feeder first and by the time you have baited the hook many of the maggots will have wriggled free from the feeder. In very warm weather the feeder should be dipped momentarily in the water immediately prior to casting which makes them less active and less likely to escape too quickly.

Each cast should be made into the same spot, the idea being to place the loose maggots into a confined area. This results in the tench remaining in the swim longer and thereby increasing your chances. Immediately the feeder touches bottom gently wind in the slack line until you can feel the feeder. The rod is then placed in two rests and a

A 4¾-lb tench taken from a gravel-pit

bobbin clipped to the line between the reel and butt ring.

Bites will vary but the most common ones are these. The bobbin may shoot upwards fast finally slamming against the rod; it may move up slowly, sometimes jerking as it does so, sometimes not; it may move upwards about an inch several times (these bites are known as 'twitchers' and occur more in autumn than in summer) or the bobbin may drop back towards the ground (when the fish is swimming towards you).

Float fishing at night If fishing at close range, this is a very exciting method. Use a float with an orange top, shotted so that about 2 inches protrudes above the water. Place a powerful torch on the ground so that the beam *just misses* the surface of the water. This is important, for it must not shine into it. Cast, and pull the float into the beam. The float will shine like a star. When making a fresh cast, do not move the torch; always pull the float into the beam. Nowadays, luminous floats are available, and are extremely effective.

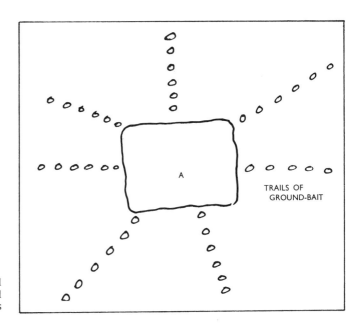

TRAILS OF
GROUND-BAIT

A

Round-the-clock ground
baiting. A denotes cleared
area among the weeds

Pre-baiting

If you wish to bait a spot for several days before fishing,
be careful. Make sure that no one sees you doing it; otherwise you will do the baiting and they the fishing!

The method adopted by the Taylors and called 'round
the clock' is, perhaps, the best. After a swim has been
selected, it is given a good dragging. Soaked bread mixed up
into a soggy mess is all right, and brandlings can be added
to this if considered desirable. A large quantity is thrown
into the swim, followed by several handfuls in a straight
line, leading away from it. This is continued in several
directions until trails of ground-bait branch out away from
the swim. The idea is that tench will eventually discover
one of these 'trails' and commence looking around to see
where it leads to. They arrive at the actual swim containing much more ground-bait, and remain there to feed. This
baiting up is continued for several days, and is often well
worth the trouble.

Playing a tench in
shallow water. If the rod
is held low the danger of
the fish splashing on the
surface is lessened.

10 Carp

by FRED TAYLOR

Description and location

There are several varieties of carp which have been produced by selective breeding on the Continent over a great
many years, but basically they all stem from the Common
Carp, which has been established in this country for a long
time.

The native Common Carp is a fast and powerful fish,
fully scaled and of semi-streamlined appearance. Its
domesticated counterpart, the King Carp, is deeper, fatter,
slower to move, but equally powerful. The scale counts
are identical.

The remaining varieties of carp are the Leather Carp (a
virtually scaleless fish with a leathery skin) and the Mirror
Carp (a fish with scales of uneven shape and very uneven
distribution). Both varieties were originally produced
through selective breeding, and as time passes, the progeny
of these fish tend to revert to the common scaling. All carp
have four barbules with the exception of the Crucian Carp,
which is a different species and has none.

Most recognized carp waters are still waters. Carp are
caught in rivers, especially those which have a steady flow,
but generally speaking, serious carp fishing is only practised
in pools, lakes, canals, and old-established sand-pits or
gravel-pits.

There is no great problem involved in locating carp in most recognized carp waters. Where the water is vast and very deep it is an extremely difficult task, and one on which I would hesitate to advise, but the problem in most carp waters is one of catching and not of location! Carp are creatures of habit and tend to follow the same paths and the same patterns of behaviour day after day, though local conditions of weather and water temperature may sometimes affect these paths and patterns to a greater or lesser extent.

In hot weather carp may be seen basking in the soft surface weed and lily beds, or cruising slowly around the marginal rushes. Sometimes these fish are feeding, more often they are not; but there is always a chance of catching a carp you can see.

Where no carp are visible, their likely feeding places may be located in a number of ways. The most reliable sign is the presence of large sheets of bubbles rising to the surface, caused by carp feeding diligently on the bottom and often accompanied by a clouding or muddying of the water.

Broken rush stems, lying like felled trees in the margins; channels through the soft silkweed beds, and uprooted soft-weed are also reliable signs of the presence of carp. The ability to recognize these signs, plus the application of any available local knowledge, will soon make it certain

A 26-lb mirror carp, caught by Tony Fordham (*right*)

whether carp are or are not present. Once located, they may be caught, if stealth and caution are practised.

Tackle

THE ROD: 10 feet, two joints, fibreglass throughout, with an action similar to a Mark IV.
THE LINE: 150 yards of 10 lb. b.s.
THE REEL: Fixed-spool.
TERMINAL TACKLE: A hook, nothing else!

Feeding habits

As carp are creatures of habit, it will pay the angler to remember this when he sets out to catch them. The fact that they follow certain patterns is a great advantage when it comes to educating them into taking hook-baits. This is the most difficult part of carp fishing. One would expect that a feeding carp would not be at all particular about what it ate, but in fact its inborn caution causes it to treat all unnatural-looking items of food with suspicion. It takes a very long time for a carp, seeing bread for the first time in its life, to accept it as food. More often than not small fish (which almost invariably infest carp lakes) have whittled it away and devoured it before the carp has had a chance to inspect it. Where waters are heavily fished, however, the carp eventually learn that bread is food and become accustomed to finding it in the margins and on the bottom. Once they have learned this, they have become catchable carp, and it is usually only a matter of time before the hook-bait is taken.

Waters which are not fished regularly must be 'fed' with bread and other baits until the carp have learned to accept them. Often it takes a long time, but it is necessary if carp are to be caught.

Where the problem of small fish is ever present, it becomes necessary to use a bait which is immune to their attentions and yet still palatable to the carp. The most successful bait in this respect is a boiled potato. Some anglers prefer them half-boiled, and very few anglers are agreed to the size, but I am a firm believer in using potatoes which are at least golfball size. I cook them in the skin until they are soft enough for me to eat myself, and I am convinced that carp prefer them that way too.

Another good bait which proves immune to the attentions of small fish is a freshwater mussel. The whole of the inside may be used; the large 'meaty' part as hook-bait, the thin, stringy pieces as ground-bait.

Carp feed on the surface as well as the bottom, so it must be decided whether they are going to be fished for with floating baits or baits lying on the bottom, at night or during the day.

Pre-baiting It must also be decided whether to use orthodox bread baits such as paste, flake, or crust, or baits which are immune to small fish, such as potatoes or mussels.

Whatever the decision, it will pay the angler to introduce these baits at intervals for a fortnight or so before fishing. Floating crusts in the margins or soft-weed beds will be found by small fish and attacked industriously. The activity around these crusts will cause the carp to take interest and finally to eat some for themselves.

The same applies to bottom baits, especially if they are introduced with the addition of a mashy substance such as bread and meal of one kind or another. After a time, the carp will begin to *expect* to find food in these places and will make regular excursions in search of more.

These pre-baiting activities are not *absolutely* essential, but I am convinced that they increase one's chances of success enormously.

Weather conditions Carp are affected by changes in water temperature and weather conditions, and the best laid schemes can go astray if this is not taken into consideration. It is difficult to lay down hard and fast rules, but it is as well to remember that carp are lovers of warm water. They are therefore unlikely to be found in very shallow water if the night is clear and cold. They are often attracted to the sun's first rays in the morning, particularly if the water in that area is shallow. Shallow water warms up quickly during the day and cools quickly during the night when the weather is settled.

Bottom fishing Having therefore chosen the pitch and pre-baited it accordingly, it only remains to place a baited hook in the same area and await results. Let us deal with bottom fishing first. The best results are likely to be obtained either during the night or very early morning. Waters which are

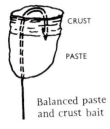

CRUST

PASTE

Balanced paste
and crust bait

not disturbed may fish well on into the day on occasions, but not as a rule.

Hook-baits such as breadpaste, honey-paste, flake, mussels, etc., may be fished on completely leadless tackles. Where crust is used it may be necessary to pinch a shot on to the line a few inches above it to ensure that it sinks. Alternatively, extra weight may be added in the form of paste moulded round the shank of the hook. This method of baiting is often necessary in waters where the bottom is covered with very soft mud or silkweed. It is referred to as 'balanced crust', and only sufficient paste to cause the crust to sink very slowly should be added.

Potatoes should be threaded on to the line with a baiting needle or a large darning needle stuck into a wooden handle as shown, before tying on the hook. After pulling the hook into the potato, the skin should be removed. When the bait has been cast, the rod should be set in rests and pointed in the general direction of the bait. The rod point should be tilted downwards towards the water (in windy conditions the tip can be completely immersed to eliminate line drag) and the rests should allow for complete and unhindered passage of the line. The clutch of the reel should be set so that it gives line on the strike. A carp will often run 20 yards when it takes the bait, but there are times when it will only run a few feet before dropping it. Specialized methods of dealing with these twitching bites are continually being considered by expert carp anglers, but for a start I believe it pays to wait for a decisive run off before striking.

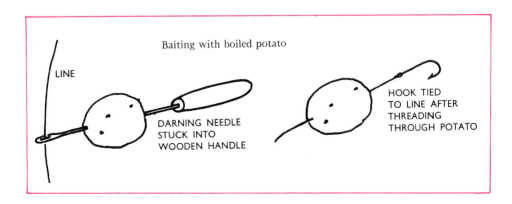

Baiting with boiled potato

LINE

DARNING NEEDLE
STUCK INTO
WOODEN HANDLE

HOOK TIED
TO LINE AFTER
THREADING
THROUGH POTATO

As the sun sets, the author settles down to an all-night carp session
(*Photograph: Tony Fordham*)

When the line is running out steadily, it usually means that the carp has taken the bait boldly, and this sort of bite may be struck with a great degree of confidence. Hold the rod and, if possible, try to judge the direction the carp is taking. Engage the pick-up and strike with a sweeping motion, far back over the shoulder. This will set the hook and cause the clutch to slip slightly immediately contact is made. It is important to ensure that the clutch is not set too loosely, or the hook will not be driven home. There is also a big chance of breakage if it is set too tightly, so it is essential that the clutch be studied and handled frequently, until it is completely understood.

Surface baits   I do not know of a more exciting form of fishing than surface fishing for carp. The number of times one's heart stops beating as a carp noses the crust, swims round it, flicks it with its tail before finally accepting or rejecting it, have to be experienced to be believed. With this type of fishing (one which can also be practised in the heat of the day with every chance of success) one watches the bait and sees the fish take it. The difficulty lies in keeping calm and waiting for the carp to swim off. The tendency is always to strike too soon and pull the hook out of the carp's mouth, but once this is overcome there is no more positive way of carp fishing.

Crust pieces the size of a match-box are used both as hook-baits and free offerings, and the same tackle is used as for bottom fishing. The crust is cast so that it settles close to the rushes or soft-weed beds. Sooner or later it will be seen and attacked by small fish, and these give an indication of what is happening. When all activity around the crust ceases, it is fairly safe to assume that a carp is in the vicinity. Sometimes, it takes the crust immediately; sometimes it will swim around it for an hour or more.

There is nothing the angler can do, except keep very still and wait. Once a carp has been scared by a shadow, or made suspicious by an unnatural movement of the bait, it will *not* return. Everything depends upon convincing the carp that all is well, and this can only be done by stealth and cunning.

A knowledge of the carp's habits, a degree of patience, and sensible tackle with which to land the fish, are the only requirements really necessary in carp fishing, as more and more anglers are learning each year.

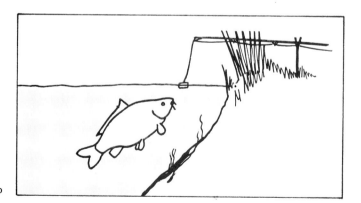

Crust fishing for carp

Opposite: An angler putting maximum side-strain on a fish. A fine study in playing a fish

11 Perch

Description and location

The perch is one of our most beautiful fish. Broad-shouldered, a big, spiky dorsal fin, large eyes, and big mouth, plus five black bars running down each flank, make it attractive.

At one time widely distributed but in recent years they have 'disappeared' from many waters. There are signs, however, that in some waters they may be returning.

If I were asked to introduce someone to angling, I would take him perch fishing. The perch is a powerful fighter, a bold biter, and will accept a large variety of baits. Also – and this is important to the newcomer – perch fishing does not require the concentration associated with bream, roach, etc., although it is not a stupid fish by any means.

Like pike, perch prefer cover under which to hide and are also found in the weir pools. You can often see that perch are feeding when they chase small fry such as bleak. All you see is a bleak jumping across the river, followed by a sucking sound behind it. This continues until the bleak is finally captured – usually against the bank.

Perch tend to shoal around November and inhabit swims such as 'onion-beds'. In these they lie up, waiting for food.

I cannot say too much about lake fishing in winter, as I do not fish them for perch. Nevertheless, I suggest the deeper water be given preference.

Tackle

THE ROD: As for roach.
THE LINE: 5 lb. b.s.
THE REEL: Fixed-spool.
TERMINAL TACKLE: A paternoster on rare occasions. Usually a shot or shots on the line suffices.

Weir fishing in summer

At the start of the season, perch will be found in great numbers in the weir-pools. A live minnow 'trotted down' on light tackle is a deadly method, or failing that, a gudgeon or bleak.

Before fishing I like to throw several handfuls of groundbait over the pool, especially in the slacker water. This attracts the small fry, which in turn attract the perch. When you see the fry scatter, cast your bait into the spot.

A Kennet perch which lifted its tail at the right moment

The float can be either an Avon or a small piece of cork, plugged so that the bait is about 3 feet below it. A swan shot is pinched on the line 12 inches from a No. 8 hook, which is passed through the top lip of the minnow.

Start by casting under the 'sill', allowing the minnow to swim downstream on the edge of the fast water. Don't get disheartened if the first cast or two fails to bring a bite; probably the perch could not reach the bait in time. Give a dozen casts at least, letting the minnow search all the pool, not forgetting the shallows.

Bites are definite, the float going straight under. When using minnows, do not delay the strike. With bleak and gudgeon, however, give the perch time to turn the bait.

Legering in wide rivers in summer
A bleak or gudgeon is best, fished on a straightforward leger. The weight is stopped 12 inches from a No. 6 hook.

Scatter several handfuls of ground-bait over the river, cast the bait into the area, and put the rod down, with the pick-up off, allowing the bait to swim around at will. When the perch takes, the line will tighten up, but again give him time to turn the bait.

Small streams in autumn

With the approach of winter, the perch shoal up, and big bags are frequently taken. I like fishing the streams which were full of 'onions' in summer, and which have now turned brown, but not completely died off.

An Avon float is used, which carries one swan shot. Use two if the stream demands it, but as a rule little is running at this time of year. Bait is either lobs or brand-lings, depending upon the colour of the water; if it is clear, use brandlings, if dirty, lobs.

Throw a few samples of the hook-bait in *as close to the rushes as possible,* and upstream of them. Adjust the float so that the bait just trips bottom. If I am using brandlings, I like two on a No. 12 hook, one on a No. 8.

Cast at the top end of the rushes and allow the worm to. trip downstream *right against the rushes.* This is important. You must, of course, be prepared to lose some tackle while 'trotting down' close to the rushes, but it is essential that your bait floats in and out of them. The perch lie up inside the rushes, merely pushing their heads out to catch food passing by. Of course you can catch perch in the 'open' waters away from the weeds, but generally speaking they are to be found close to cover.

Bites are definite, the float either going straight under, or turning towards the rushes, dipping as it does so. Wait a few seconds before striking, especially if using lobs, and get the fish away from cover and into the 'open' water quickly. There is generally no need to remain long in one swim, if bites are not forthcoming; give a swim about twenty minutes before moving on.

Lakes in winter

Lakes that hold perch will produce good fish in winter, but they are not easy to catch, mainly owing to changing temperatures. The great perch taken by Richard Walker in Arlesey Lake in the fifties were located in the 50-foot deep channel that runs across it. They were taken on legered lobworms, cast out as far as possible, and were allowed to take several yards of line before the strike was made.

A much different technique is employed in a lake close to my home. Here, the perch will not accept worms, but a small roach with which the lake abounds, fished on a single hook, and allowed to swim around, is accepted.

(Do remember, however, that live baiting is now outlawed on many waters.)

Fishing canals in winter

Many canals hold good perch. Tackle and bait are as for fishing small streams in autumn, although a minnow is sometimes preferred. As with roach, I find the majority of my canal perch feed on the 'slope' on either side of the canal, in preference to the middle. Allow the worm to drag the bottom, but if this fails, try it just off, and keep casting until you find the fish. A little 'cloud' ground-bait or a sample of hook-bait can be introduced from time to time, in an effort to attract the small fry.

The use of a paternoster

Paternoster

For as long as I can remember (and long before that) writers have recommended the use of a paternoster. I don't like them, although there are occasions, when fishing a small hole in weeds, for example, that it is useful. It should therefore get a mention.

The diagram showing how a paternoster is set up is self-explanatory. The weight of lead depends upon the current, and the swivel should be a fairly small one.

Bait a minnow on a No. 8 hook, or failing that a bleak or gudgeon on a No. 6. The bait is lowered or cast into the desired spot, and fished stationary. A small cork serves as the float, and is allowed to slide up the line, being stopped from sliding down on the swivel by a matchstick tied on the line just above it. When the bait reaches bottom the cork slides up the line, finally resting on the surface. If you wish, the cork can be taken off, and the bait simply legered.

Spinning

Voblex

Many perch are taken on spinners, an artificial bait which when retrieved, spins, imitating a small fish, and it is always advisable to carry one or two around with you. On a hot summer's day, when everything is 'off', or appears to be, a spinner cast into the right spot can be very deadly. However, I don't believe in taking an assortment of patterns, relying on a couple which have proved very successful. One is the 'Voblex', consisting of a rubber head with a small bronze spinner behind it. In the water it is very life-like, and is extremely successful for perch fishing. Don't rely on one size, but take two or three, and if one fails, try another.

The spinner is cast into the likely-looking swims, and retrieved *slowly*. Don't just wind straight in. Retrieve it jerkily, thereby giving it a bit of 'life', and search every bit of water, not forgetting under your own bank. As when pike spinning, stand well back from the bank, and use a rod at least 10 feet long.

Failing a 'Voblex', I like a natural bait, attached to a 'mount', as described in the pike chapter. A small bleak is my favourite, or failing this a minnow. If you are using a minnow, the size of the 'mount' must be scaled down, of course, a size 14 treble being about right.

Although not strictly spinning, a worm retrieved slowly through a swim is often deadly. Hook a lob through its head once with a No. 8 hook, and wind it back erratically. If, and when, the worm is seized, slacken off, and allow a few seconds before striking. I have often done this during a match, when spinning and live-baiting is, of course, barred. A perch has put in an appearance, and a worm, spun through my swim, has added to the bag.

The Queen's Pool at Blenheim

12 Pike

Description and location

Streamlined in shape, with long, pointed head, containing thousands of teeth, the pike is aptly named the 'freshwater shark'. Extremely voracious-looking, its main diet consists of fish, alive or dead, and when in the prime of condition it is a very sporting fish.

Pike fishing for me does not begin until November, although the pike is in fighting trim by June 16th. At this time of year the best sport is found in weir-pools, where the fish have moved after spawning. They will be found anywhere in the pools, but the majority have accepted my bait on the edge of the very fast water.

By November, the first frosts have arrived, the weeds are brown in colour, and the pike is forced to search for his food. In rivers, fish the swims where bulrushes ('onions') were in summer, their tops now wavering in the current, and also where rushes line the bank. Try the 'chubby' swims, where willows overhang, their roots trailing in the water, and any swim that provides cover of some sort. You can catch pike in weedless, coverless swims, but many more will be found where they can lie up out of sight.

Fish the fast water as well as the slacks and lay-bys, areas of slack water caused usually by a depression in the bank, or a cattle drink; but I don't like swims deeper than 12 feet when fishing rivers. Swims with a depth of about 5 feet appear the most productive, even in extremely cold conditions.

In lakes and ponds, the pike tend to frequent certain areas, both deep and shallow. Location is largely by trial and error, but any area of a lake where died-off 'onions' can be seen is worth trying. Search the water thoroughly and keep your eyes open for swirls or small fish leaping.

In rough weather, fish just outside the rush beds. Wind blowing the rushes drives the pike from cover for they dislike wavering rushes brushing against their flanks.

Tackle THE ROD : As for carp.

THE LINE : For general fishing a 10 lb. b.s. For dead-baits a 12 lb. b.s.

THE REEL : Fixed-spool.

TERMINAL TACKLE : This depends upon the method and is described later.

A BAITING NEEDLE.

Baiting needle

Summer piking At this time of year the weir-pools are the best bet, and the method described in the perch chapter applies here, except that the hook is attached to wire. This consists of several strands of extremely fine wire twisted together, which, if of the best quality, is extremely supple. Apart from this variation in equipment, tactics and tackle are the same.

Trotting down in winter This is a sadly neglected method, which is a pity, for it is extremely effective. I should emphasize, however, that it is a method suited only to medium-paced waters.

I like small baits up to 7 inches in length, gudgeon or chub if possible. Hooks are No. 6 on wire and are attached to the line by means of a swivel. A bullet about $3/8$ inch in diameter is stopped by a shot 12 inches above the bait. A piece of bored cork, plugged so that the bait swims about 18 inches off bottom, completes the outfit.

Before setting up your tackle, throw several handfuls of 'cloud' ground-bait along the reach of river being fished; this attracts the small fry, which in turn attract the pike. Keep introducing handfuls of ground-bait while fishing. You *can* catch pike without it, but you will catch many more with it.

Fred Towns spins a dead bait for pike at Blenheim, close to the famous beech trees

Cast under your own bank, and allow the bait to swim down for about thirty yards, then retrieve it *slowly;* cast out a little farther, and repeat. Unless fishing very wide rivers, you will eventually finish up under the far bank. Then move down to the end of the 'beat', and start all over again. It is a matter of choice whether you remain in one place and pay off line, or walk down the bank. I prefer the latter course, except for the initial cast under my own bank, when to walk down might put the pike away.

Bites will not be difficult to detect. Usually the cork suddenly disappears, but it will sometimes slide gradually under. There are occasions, however, when you think the tackle is snagged, the cork remaining in one position partially submerged. If this occurs, do not snatch at it; simply take up the slack line and gradually pull. If it is a pike, it will soon move off.

Bites usually follow the same pattern; the float moves off for a few yards and then stops. A series of jerks then take place, these being caused by the pike turning the bait round head first, before swallowing, having grabbed it across the back when it first 'struck'. When the bait has been turned the float moves off again, and continues moving, usually upstream. Now take up the slack line (this is important), and drive the hook home with a good firm pull, followed by a second pull, just to make sure.

Pike do not always behave in this manner. Sometimes the cork will go under, remaining in that position until you strike. Or it may move off and keep going, the bait being swallowed immediately, but as a rule this occurs when the bait is a very small one. When these different bites occur, you must use your own judgment as to when the strike should be made, and this only comes with experience.

Dead-bait fishing A great many pike have fallen to dead-baits, especially herring or mackerel which can be used either in whole or in half. A powerful rod will be necessary for casting such baits and the line should be about 12 lb b.s. To mount a half-bait, get 15 inches of wire (I recommend Berkely's 'Steelstrand') and attach a No 2 single hook on one end with another about three inches above it. This is done by crimping, using a pair of crimping pliers and brass 'sleeves'. Now push one single LIGHTLY through the skin of the bait at the 'thick' end, the other close to the 'wrist' of the tail. Finally, bind the wire to the herring just above the tail with fine thread which takes the force of the cast but which will break when you strike the pike. No float is used and the bait is simply legered.

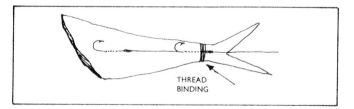

THREAD
BINDING

Mounting a half-herring. (Dead-bait!)

If you are using a roach or dace as bait, remember to puncture its air-bladder with a baiting needle before casting. Failure to do this will result in the bait rising off the bottom which is unnatural, to say the least, although pike, on occasions, will take a bait suspended in this manner. After

Pike fishing in floodwater. Note that when the fish is in danger
of becoming entangled in the rushes, the rod is pushed out at arm's
length, thereby keeping the fish out and not pulling it in

Spinning for pike. Note the angler stands well back from the
water's edge. You can't do this with a short rod

casting, place the rod between two rod rests with the pick-up of the reel open and whether using whole baits or half-baits, strike a few seconds after the pike starts taking a line: in this way you should avoid hooking it in its throat.

Several handfuls of groundbait thrown around the dead-bait can be an advantage. The small fry feeding on the groundbait swim off when the pike approaches, leaving the herring in full view.

Points to watch There are days when the pike will not feed upon the bait, merely cruising around, holding it crosswise between its jaws. After much experimenting, however, I have discovered that on such days they *will* feed, but only require a very small bait to satisfy their hunger. This usually occurs after a period of high water, when the pike have gorged themselves with food. After all, when we have had a dinner we don't want another straight away, but will accept a chocolate! On these occasions I catch a number

This big Blenheim pike was taken by Malcolm Dore on a bleak bait

of small bleak, and when a bite occurs I let the pike go well away before striking. Strangely enough, the pike, even if in the 10 lb. class, is not badly hooked, the hook usually going home in the corner of the mouth.

On the other hand, on a day immediately after flood-water has gone down, and the pike are starved, they will take any bait within reason. On such occasions you should strike quickly, especially if using small baits, otherwise the hook or hooks will be swallowed, and result in the destruction of the pike.

Spinning

Weather and water conditions determine the type of spinner suitable for the occasion, and the manner in which it is fished. I do not think a pike prefers one type of spinner to another just because it is a different colour. I am convinced that the shape is the attraction; not that a pike recognizes it as such, but by the vibration set up by it. The old-fashioned 'kidney' spoon (today these have been replaced by the 'Vibro' spinners which are equally as good), is most successful because, as I think, of the enormous vibration it makes while travelling in the water. The attention of the pike is aroused by the vibration, and seeing something flash by, he grabs it. A metal spoon is far more successful when the water is slightly coloured, as its sharp outlines appear blurred to the fish, whereas in clear water it is often recognised as something artificial.

Spinning with artificial bait

If you can, spin slowly. This is not always possible, of course, especially in shallow, weedy water, when a plug is best, but in fairly weed-free water I like the spinner to spin slow and deep. Also, do not retrieve it at one speed; give the reel handle two or three turns, then stop a second. This puts 'life' into the spinner. Make two casts in each swim, in case the pike missed it first time, and in cold conditions especially, spin close to the bottom.

Wobbling a natural bait

A natural bait is far more likely to succeed than the artificial. In clear water it is a 'must'. The bait, when killed, is attached to a 'flight' or 'mount'.

Attach a treble to a length of alasticum as previously described, then slide two single hooks (the size of these and the treble depends upon the size of bait; a bleak would

Dead-bait mount for wobbling

require a No 8 treble and No 6 single) down the wire. Now twist the wire four times round the shank of one single. The distance between the single and treble is important and should be such, so that when the single is in the bait's mouth, the treble is halfway between the dorsal fin and tail (see diagram). Now push this single through the bait's mouth and out of one eye, then push the other single up the wire an inch or so and through the bait's mouth coming out of the other eye. Now 'tease' the wire back through the eye of the single so the two hooks meet. Finally, push one hook of the treble lightly through the back of the bait (see diagram).

I like, if possible, to dispense with lead in any shape or form. In still waters it is seldom necessary, anyway, but in rivers a little is essential to keep the bait down deep. A small 'anti-kink' lead placed some 3 feet from the bait is all right, but always fish with as little lead as possible. When a pike grabs your dead-bait, slacken off immediately, and give it a second or two before striking. This is not easy, I know, but you soon get used to it.

You will not be able to cast a weightless dead-bait very far, but there is no need to worry. The majority of my pike grab the bait close to the bank, where they lie up under cover. Stand well back with the tip of the rod protruding over the edge of the bank. Retrieve the bait in an irregular manner; make it *look* like the dying fish, which it is supposed to represent.

When tackling-up the rod is placed on a stool, out of harm's way, *not* laid on the ground (see page 15)

13 Barbel

Description and location

The barbel is another beautiful fish. In appearance it is like a monster gudgeon, and has four 'barbels' by its mouth, two on either side of its upper jaw. The mouth is *underneath* its head, as in a shark. The fish is bronze all over, with a massive red tail. There is a sudden drop in line from its shoulders to mouth, this shape assisting it to stay in fast water, which it loves.

The barbel is not an easy fish to catch. There are many anglers who have never seen, let alone caught one, and in all fairness, there are not many rivers that hold them. The Thames, the Avon, the Kennet, and the Stour are good barbel rivers; they are found in parts of Yorkshire, notably the Swale, and are also established in the Severn. I am always pleased to catch one, however small it may be.

Barbel, as a rule, spawn quite early, and in the opening weeks of the season the most likely swims are those close to the shallows, at the 'tail' of a weir-pool. They do not usually remain there for long, however, and around August time tend to drop back to the quiet reaches of the river, or work up into the pools. During June and July, then, try the shallows below the weirs, especially during the early morning and late evening, and during the middle of the day give the pool itself a try. Make sure the bottom is reasonably free of snags, and if it is a nice, clear, gravelly one (which it usually is) so much the better. Failing the shallows, try the top of the pool in the fast water, close to the piles, and against the concrete wall. You may find some snags here, so be careful.

The Avon at Bickton, Hampshire, where the author caught three different species to order, for Jack Hargreaves' TV programme

Weir-pools are not the only places where you will find barbel. Far more barbel inhabit the 'open' river than anglers imagine, coming usually from straight, gravelly swims. Locating them is difficult, and I find mine either by seeing them jump or roll or seeing one caught. How many anglers, silently sitting on the bank, have seen a big red tail suddenly appear above the surface, and disappear without a sound! That is a barbel, and you can be sure that a shoal is very close to the spot where that tail appeared. Often, however, they leap clear of the surface, re-entering with a terrific splash. Whenever you see any of these occurrences, fish that area hard.

Many swims, of course, have a 'barbel' look about them, and if you fancy such a swim, then by all means fish it. Nice smooth glides along a clay bank, with shallows at the bottom always spell barbel.

Tackle   THE ROD: 11 feet, fibre-glass throughout, with an action similar to a Mark IV.

THE LINE: 6 lb. b.s. for legering, 5 lb. b.s. for 'trotting'.

THE REEL: Fixed-spool.

TERMINAL TACKLE: When legering, the 'sliding link'. For 'trotting', a swan shot pinched on the line 12 inches from the hook suffices, but an Arlesey bomb may be necessary in very fast water.

**Trotting down
in summer**

In the early weeks of the season 'trotting down', in and around the weir-pools, is an extremely deadly method. Bait is a minnow, alive or dead, and the best times to fish are early morning and late evening.

Get a small piece of cork, with a hole in its centre. Push this up the line, and plug it with a piece of stick. The minnow is hooked through the top lip only, and the cork set so that you are fishing 12 inches deeper than the actual depth. Cast upstream, and allow the bait to come gently downstream, tripping the bottom as it does so.

Line must be gathered up, or paid out, depending on whether the cork is coming towards you or going away, and must be kept as tight as possible. Bites, as a rule, are decisive. The cork, without warning, shoots under. Do not hesitate, but strike *at once*. Sometimes the cork will bounce along the surface, usually travelling downstream. Again, do not delay the strike. Do not allow the bait to travel downstream too quickly. If it does, increase the weight slightly or·lengthen the distance between cork and bait by a few inches.

A great number of barbel are taken 'trotting' with maggots. Use a float which carries two swan shots and stop these about 15 inches from a No. 12 hook. On this place either two or three maggots. Now set the float so that the weight *just* touches bottom, then position yourself several yards upstream of the swim. Allow the float to travel downstream to the end of the swim with as little line as possible on the water. Strike immediately the float disappears, even though this may not always be caused by a taking barbel but by the lead or hook fouling the bottom. Normally one should ground-bait with maggots, a handful introduced every ten minutes or so being sufficient to keep the barbel interested.

Legering in summer If the swim is reasonably free of snags, I like to 'roll' the bottom, and choose a weight accordingly. I do not ground-bait too heavily, a few samples of the hook-bait, plus a handful or two of soaked breadcrumbs being sufficient. Cast, and allow the bait to roll round slowly, and if the water is fast, hold the rod up high. This way, water pressure on the line is reduced, thereby keeping the bait in position better. If possible, however, hold the rod low.

If you use cheese-paste, sausage meat, or lobs, a 'trail' of 12 inches is about right, but for crust, bring the lead to within 2 inches of the hook.

Don't forget, if using a worm, to hook it *once*, not several times, and a point worth remembering is that barbel often prefer it hooked through its head and not the middle.

Barbel bites, on the leger, vary. The most common one is for the rod top to move slowly forward about 6 or 7 inches. Failing this, it will 'buzz', moving backwards and

The angler is not afraid of barbed-wire fences. If he stands well back, with the tree providing cover, the fish are not aware of his presence

forwards *very* quickly, about half an inch at a time. If you are holding the line (and you should be), it feels as if someone is sandpapering it. Now you can do two things; strike at once, or wait. If you wait, the rod will most certainly be pulled round, anything from 3 inches to 3 feet. I strike on the 'buzz', for the following reason. A barbel picks up the bait, and lying still, turns it over and over in its mouth; this causes the 'buzzing' on the rod top. Then, a second or two later it turns round downstream, which results in the rod being pulled round. I don't like delaying the strike until the barbel has got its head down and steam up! I consider it much better to strike while he is lying still, which lessens the chances of breaking your tackle.

Strike, however, at anything that moves slowly, the exception to this being if using lobs, when I like to wait for a second or third pull. But with cheese-paste, sausage meat or crust, strike at the first *slow* movement.

These are the most common types of bite, although you will get others. The line may slacken suddenly, for instance. But if in doubt, strike.

You may be fishing a swim, however, where 'rolling the bottom' is not possible owing to boulders, lumps of clay, etc. on the bottom. The bait, therefore, must be stationary, and the 'trail' a long one.

Fishing the Hampshire Avon (Royalty Fishery)

Barbel, as I have said, are difficult to catch. There is one water, however, the Royalty Fishery on the Avon, where you stand an extraordinary chance of success and if you want to catch one, this is the place. It is essential, however, that you know how to fish this water, otherwise very few will be caught.

The length of 'trail' is most important. Instead of 12 inches, you want one of 3 feet, or even longer! I found the 'sliding link' very satisfactory, as the lead is inclined to become entangled in the boulders that are along the river. If this happens, only the lead is lost, which can be important if a barbel is on the other end!

The most popular swims on the Royalty are the 'Piles', 'Railway Bridge', and 'Pipe Bridge', but any swim containing a 'salmon-stone' is worth trying. A 'salmon-stone' is a big boulder behind which the salmon lie, and there are many throughout the fishery. A 'salmon stone' is detected by the water 'boiling' on the surface as it hits the boulder, and you position yourself several feet above it. Cast so that your lead hits the water level with the stone, and several feet away from it, towards midstream. Hold the rod up high, and allow your bait to roll round so that it comes to rest *just* behind the stone. The lead is resting against the stone, and providing the rod is held high, the bait will remain in position. Bites will be as I described earlier.

The Avon is also full of streamer weed in summer, and the barbel love to get under it! You can fish in this weed quite easily in the following manner.

Fish, if possible, upstream and adjust your weight to *just* hold bottom. Cast into the weed, and allow the bait to sink on a fairly tight line. The bait will eventually work its way through the weed, and the rod should be held high. Bites will, as a rule, be 'slack-line' ones, the line falling flat upon the water. Strike if it does so, and you should hook your fish. If you don't, the next time strike in the normal manner, then quickly take up the slack line and strike again, in fact striking twice. This takes a bit of practice, but is not so difficult as it sounds. Although this is the most common type of bite, you do get others. A light tightening of the line will take place, or a knock on the rod top will be felt. Strike all these at once.

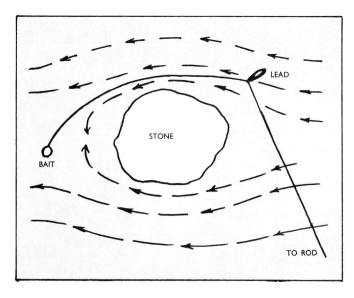

Fishing behind a
salmon stone

Fishing the Hampshire Avon. The author makes a fine catch with the first cast of the day (*Photograph: Tony Fordham*)

If you hook a fish in this streamer weed, or if one takes you into it while playing it, pull on the barbel from down-stream, *not* up. You can pull a fish through the densest streamer weed from downstream, but you can't from upstream, a point worth remembering.

The size of bait is important when fishing the Avon. Cheese-paste is very good, and before the sun becomes really hot, pieces the size of a walnut can be used. As the day gets hotter, reduce the size of your bait, until you are using pieces hazel-nut size on a No. 10 hook. As it becomes cooler again, increase the size, until you are again using big pieces when darkness falls. Don't forget to increase the hook size as well.

Maggots, fished on small hooks, are also effective. Large quantities (at least half a gallon) are essential as ground-bait, which are best introduced via a bait-dropper. A bait-dropper is a plastic tube or box, devised so that the bottom opens when the dropper touches the river bed, and the contents are released. There are several variations of bait-dropper. Pack the dropper with maggots; then gently lower it into the swim. Immediately the dropper opens, drop your baited hook into the swim, for a bite will often occur immediately afterwards. To save time, the dropper is best used on a spare rod.

Slacks and eddies behind patches of streamer weed appear to be the best swims. Bunch the weight about 12 inches from the hook, and set the float so that it lies at half-cock. Should this fail, adjust it slightly so that the bait travels around the eddy just off bottom. Bites are determined by the float quickly disappearing from sight.

For a period, maggots were banned on this water as the constant introduction of gallons of maggots concentrated the barbel into the slacks, which made fishing the fast runs virtually a waste of time. Recently, however, the ban was lifted.

Care must be taken when playing barbel. They fight very strongly indeed, and do not be led into thinking one is finished when it finally turns over. They have a habit of coming to life again, and with a flick of their great tails, bore down again towards the bottom. This flick of the tail spells danger if it catches your line, and is the cause of many breakages, just when the angler is congratulating himself.

The author with a hundred and thirty pounds of Thames bream

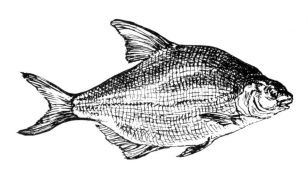

14 Bream

Description and location

Bream are widespread throughout the country and are found in both rivers and still-waters. For the really big bream, still-waters are generally best, especially gravel-pits. Here, however, they are very difficult and I advise the beginner to keep to rivers.

Bream are big, flat-sided fish and there are two varieties, bronze and silver. The latter variety is rare, although most bream up to about 4lb. in weight are silver when caught. When retained in keepnets, however, this silver vanishes, being replaced by a slight bronze.

Bream are shoal fish. Where you catch one, there are many more. Yet a bream is a puzzling fish. One day fish after fish will come to the net, yet twenty-four hours later, under apparently ideal conditions, you can't get a bite.

But it can be a most obliging fish, and big bags are frequently caught. I have taken many 100 lb. bags at a time, and in gravel-pits many big fish between $10\frac{1}{4}$ and 8 lbs.

Location is often difficult. In summer the best way is to watch until they 'roll' on the surface. A big brown back appears, followed by a black tail, thrashing the surface as it disappears. Often a series of swirls will appear, and a novice is apt to say 'Pike!'; but it will be bream all right. Rolling and swirling may take place in one particular spot, or over an area of a hundred yards or more, as the shoal moves up or down river. A moving shoal is difficult to pin down and is discussed later in the chapter. In small, clear streams the water will turn brown when bream are feeding, as the fish stir up the bottom. When this occurs, fish in the 'dirty' water.

There are occasions, however, when these visible signs

A catch of Thames bream. The best fish, one of 6 lb., held by the author

do not appear. You may think the bream are 'off' and you can fish all day and not find them, but I have caught good bags on such occasions, usually with the assistance of some friends.

Four or five of us fish, and we will call ourselves A, B, C, and D. We space ourselves out at twenty-yard intervals, and fish for about fifteen minutes. If, by this time, no bites have occurred, A moves down beyond D and we fish again for ten minutes. B then moves down beyond A and so on. In this way, a lot of water is covered, and at any time one of us may locate the bream. If one does, the rest close in on him, all fishing the same swim until the fish go off.

Bream are reputed to be lovers of deep holes, but this is not always so. In summer they tend to inhabit swims containing 'cabbages'; not always right in them, but very close.

We are also told that they prefer slack water, yet I catch many big bags in weir-pools. One in particular holds an

immense head of fish, and location here is not difficult.
They inhabit one spot only (just on the 'tail'), and if any-
one asks me for a day's 'breaming', I take him there.

The above remarks apply to summer fishing. Location in
winter is somewhat easier, for the fish tend to inhabit
certain swims, where they remain until March.

Many of my favourite swims at this time of year are no
more than 3 feet in depth, and I have caught bream from
such places in blinding snow-storms. These shallow swims,
however, are usually close to a deep hole, where I suspect
the fish lie up before or after feeding. I do catch them in
the holes, but in floodwater especially it is on the shallows
that they feed most.

A swim that yielded bream consistently in summer is
also worth trying in winter, especially if it contained
'cabbages'. They may not be in the exact swim, but are
often very close to it, so keep moving about until you find
them.

Lock cuttings should be tried, especially when the river
is in flood. In normal conditions they are not so productive.

Tackle THE ROD : As for roach.
THE LINE : 5 lb. b.s. for float fishing, 6 lb. b.s. for legering.
THE REEL : Fixed-spool.
TERMINAL TACKLE : For legering, the 'sliding link', or
  Arlesey Bombs direct to line. For float fishing, a running
  bullet, stopped by a shot the required distance from the
  hook.

Legering in summer in wide rivers Bream fishing at this time of year calls for a very large
supply of ground-bait. Buy as much as you can afford, and
take it dry. I like to take two canvas bucketsful and that
often isn't enough! You *must* have ground-bait; without it
you might just as well stay at home.

Having located the bream, throw in two big handfuls of
ground-bait. Tackle up with the 'sliding link', and have the
lead 12 inches from the hook, which is a No. 10 tied direct
to line. Start with two swan shots and use paste as bait;
failing this try cheesepaste. Brandlings can also be tried if
paste fails.

Cast out over the ground-bait, wait until the bait hits
bottom, and take up any slack line *quickly*. Bites may take

place immediately, for bream do not hang about when feeding.

Bites are as follows. Usually the rod top goes round slowly about 2 inches, or it may give a small pull of about an inch, followed immediately by another. Or, after tightening up the line, the rod may jerk backwards remaining in that position. It may give a sharp jerk, and nothing more. All these bites must be struck immediately. If the fish is missed, which rarely happens, wait for a second, or sometimes third, pull.

Not all bites will be seen on the rod top. Bream often take a bait as it is sinking, and if you watch the line immediately the bait hits the water, you will see it moving up and down in the water. Strike! Sometimes you have already tightened up the line, and while you are watching the rod top, the line suddenly hangs loose. Strike this, but if you miss, wait for it to tighten up again.

If using brandlings, do not strike at the first movement of the rod top or line, but wait for a second pull.

If bites are slow in coming, take off one of the swan shots. The bait will sink more slowly, and if the bream are taking a sinking bait, watch the line, not the rod top.

Keep up the supply of ground-bait, two big handfuls at a time after catching each fish, certainly every five minutes. If you don't, the bream will soon move on.

Cast accurately. Even though the bream may be widely scattered, they appear to feed in a very small area.

Legering in weir-pools Bream like fast water. If you know of a pool containing bream, they usually remain there throughout the season, feeding in one particular area.

Swim feeder

Tactics as before, although one Arlesey Bomb is often preferable to the 'sliding link', especially if a very long cast is called for. Ground-bait *must* be heavy, as heavy as possible. Again take plenty.

Should you experience difficulty in getting the ground-bait to sink in the desired spot in fast water then a 'swim-feeder' can be used. The best type of swim-feeder is made by Peter Drennan and is available in three different sizes. The feeder is prevented from slipping on to the hook by means of a plastic leger stop. Ground-bait, which should not be too heavy, is then forced into the 'swim-feeder'.

The cast is made in the normal manner.

This method ensures the ground-bait is lying close to the hook-bait and providing it is the required consistency, the ground-bait should filter out gradually through the holes. When a fresh cast is made the 'swim-feeder' is refilled.

Float fishing in summer

You can if you wish use a float, provided long casting is not necessary. Try an Avon with a shot loading of one or two swan shots which are set 15 inches from the hook, the float set so that the bait JUST trips bottom. Groundbait as before; bait, crust or brandlings.

Usually the float slides straight under; failing that, it may sink lower in the water, remaining in that position; it may travel downstream faster than it should, or it may go upstream. If you are using crust, strike immediately, but with brandlings wait a second or two. If no bites are forthcoming, move the float down gradually until the bait is finally at mid-water, also vary the length of 'trail'. Keep experimenting until you get results.

Maggots are also successful, especially in the autumn, varying in numbers from two on a No. 14 hook, to a dozen on a No. 8. I find, however, that bunches of maggots tend to clog the hook, resulting in fish becoming unhooked. And as large quantities are necessary for ground-bait, it becomes an expensive business, so stick to crust and worms.

Float fishing in winter ('stret-pegging')

Stret-pegging is described on page 32 and results at this time of year are best obtained during a period of high and coloured water. Use a float that carries a 'barley-corn' lead about an inch in length, which is stopped about 12 inches above the hook. The best bait is brandlings.

There is no need for large quantities of ground-bait, but take enough. Two big handfuls to start with is all right, with further handfuls at about fifteen-minute intervals.

Find the depth of the swim, set the float, and then push it *up* another 2 feet (this distance between your float and hook is now of course 2 feet more than the actual depth). Cast slightly outwards of the swim, allowing your float and bait to swing into it, the line between rod top and float being kept tight. When the bait reaches the desired spot, it should remain there with the float half-cocked.

Bites usually consist of the float sliding out towards

midstream, at the same time gradually going under. Wait until it disappears and tighten – there is no need to strike. Failing this, the float will fall flat, and move either outwards or downstream, remaining flat.

When the water is clear and back to normal, slightly different tactics are necessary. This is one of the rare occasions when I enthuse over maggots, but, unlike summer fishing, you do not require a lot; a few handfuls mixed in with the ground-bait are sufficient.

Tactics are more or less as before, except that maggots are the hook-bait – three on a No. 12 being my favourite. Take some coloured ones; often the fish prefer a red to a white maggot, and I usually have two white and one red on the hook.

The same types of bite will occur, also one that gives a sharp pluck on the float, and which, if the rod is being held (as it should be), is also felt on the line. This should be struck immediately, and you usually connect; but if you do begin missing them, wait for a more definite pull.

Fishing an eddy

I don't believe in fishing eddies too often; far more of my bream come from the straight, fast stretches. However, they are worth a try at times, especially in very cold weather.

Tackle is as for 'stret-pegging', and set the float so that the lead just trips bottom. Shot the float so that about an inch protrudes above the water, cast, and let out a little slack line. Allow the float to turn round and round in the eddy, on a fairly taut line. There is no mistaking the bite; the float will gently slide under, or lift slightly. Again, maggots are best, or brandlings if the water is coloured. If this fails, push the float up a little so that it half-cocks, and hold it on a taut line.

15 Eels

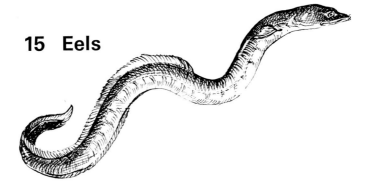

Description and location

The eel does not require much description. Its shape is that of a snake and it has a fairly small mouth and small red eyes. The colouring of an eel appears to depend upon the water in which it lives. Those on gravel have yellowish undersides, and I have caught them silver in colour. Very few waters do *not* hold eels, yet few anglers fish for them. A pity, for they are fine sporting fish.

I like eel fishing, especially at night, and one can afford to relax at this game, as there is little need for concentration. To hook a big eel is a wonderful experience, and I spend many a summer's day or night fishing for them.

Eels are found anywhere in rivers and lakes, but certain swims are better than others. In rivers, I like the deep holes, especially in the weir-pools, and in lakes I go for the deepest water I can find. Failing these swims, wherever a lot of rubbish has accumulated is good, as are 'onions' and 'cabbages'.

Night fishing if allowed, is best, when the eels move more freely. A nice mild night is the time to be out, or if in daytime choose a close, humid day. Eels do *not* bite better in thunderstorms, despite claims to the contrary, but I have taken good bags immediately following one. They are primarily a summer fish, and will feed in the hottest weather, but night fishing is the most productive.

Tackle

THE ROD : For eels you *must* have a fairly powerful rod. A fibre-glass one, 10 feet in length is about right.
THE REEL : Fixed-spool.
THE LINE : 10 lb. b.s.
TERMINAL TACKLE : A 'barley-corn' lead, hook.
A BAITING NEEDLE.

Legering Eels take most baits offered them, but for the big ones a dead fish cannot be bettered, bleak and gudgeon being the best. Lobs are all right, but tend to attract the small eels (boot-laces), which should be avoided.

Get your dead-bait, insert the baiting needle into its mouth, bringing it out again at the fork of its tail. There should be about an inch of needle protruding from either end of the bait. Now get the 'barley-corn lead', thread the wire hook through it and allow the lead to drop down to the hook shank. Push the loop of the wire through the eye of the needle, and pull the needle right through the bait until the lead rests against the bait's mouth. Remove the needle from the wire, and with the eye of the needle ram the lead down the bait's throat, out of sight. Pull the loop of the wire until the hook is inside the bait's mouth, with the bend of it outside the mouth. The hook, plus bait, is now attached to the line in the normal manner and is ready for casting. A small point worth remembering here is to prick the bait all over with the baiting needle. This allows the flavours of the bait to 'scent' the water. The eel picks up the scent, eventually finding the bait.

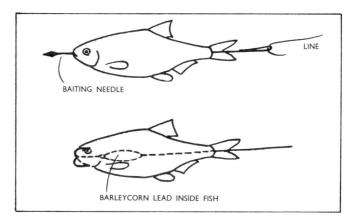

Threading dead bait for eels

That is how I thread my baits, but if you do not like wire (and many don't) you can attach the bait in the following manner: push the needle in at the tail and out at the mouth. Thread the line through the eye of the needle, pull through, and remove the needle. The end of the line is now protruding from the mouth of the bait. Thread the lead on the line, attach an eyed hook, and pull back as above. A split shot is now pinched on the line against the tail of the bait. This prevents the eel spitting the bait up the line when hooked, and biting off the hook. The bait, being fixed in this manner, also forces the mouth of the eel open, partially choking it. These are two methods of attaching the bait; use whichever you prefer.

Long casting is often necessary, especially in weir-pools and lakes, and a bait with the lead inside it greatly improves casting range.

Bite-indicators I generally use an electric bite alarm when eel fishing. Bite alarms first came into prominence when night carp fishing became popular. Many anglers make their own and because of this there are many 'variations on an original theme'. For the electrically-minded, the building of an alarm is quite simple, but for those, like me, who are not that way inclined, one must be bought.

The most popular bite alarm in use today is the Optonic. The alarm is attached to a brass rod or something similar and pushed into the ground at the water's edge. A rod rest, which supports the rod handle, is then positioned three or four feet behind.

Bites are detected by the buzzer being activated as the line is pulled by the fish. Further description is unnecessary as full instructions are supplied with the alarm.

Bites follow the same pattern. The line will run out for several yards, then stop, and for a minute or two, knocks are felt on the line. This is followed by another fast run. Allow the eel to run several yards, close the pick-up, *take up any slack line* and strike. Having hooked the eel, you 'pump' him in, which is done in the following manner.

Pull the rod right back into a vertical position, then quickly point the rod at the fish, *at the same time winding in*, thus keeping the line tight. Then, holding the line tight, pull the rod back until vertical, and repeat. Continue pumping until the eel is at the bank, and then net it, or, if the bank is level with the water, slide it out.

Fishing weirs When fishing weirs, and if much water is coming through, false bites, caused by floating debris, often occur. Under such conditions, in daylight I dispense with the indicator, and hold the rod upright, with as much line out of the water as possible. Constant flicking of the line will be necessary in order to avoid and to free rubbish, and when this happens eel fishing is not so relaxing as it can be.

You may also be fishing with your bait very close to a snag or snags. The eel will pick up the bait, run a few feet, become tangled and feeling resistance, drop it. If this occurs, a miniature snap tackle similar to the one described for mounting a herring (in the Pike chapter) using No. 10 trebles, can be used, a single hook going in at the bait's mouth, with a treble halfway down its flank. The bait, of course, is not threaded. When the eel commences to run, strike, and although it is not certain that the fish will be hooked, at least you have a chance, and this is the only way to make the best of a poor job.

16 Other species

RUDD
Description and location

The rudd is a very beautiful fish indeed, very similar to the roach. Its fins, however, are much darker, its flanks golden and its lower lip overlaps the top one – the opposite of the roach, with which it is often confused.

It is found primarily in still waters, and often in very large waters. Rudd feed more freely in summer, although they are worth seeking in winter during a mild spell. They will be found at all depths depending upon conditions, and during hot weather will feed profusely on the surface.

Tackle

As for roach.

Tactics

The same as described for tench will usually be successful. Failing these, a floating crust, as mentioned in the carp chapter, with a scaling down of tackle, is extremely deadly, when the fish can be seen moving on the surface.

DACE
Description and location

Similar to a chub, for which it is often mistaken. The best method of identification is the anal fin (the one nearest the tail), which is concave, whereas that of a chub is convex.

A chub and a dace, showing the difference in anal fins
Top: chub fin convex
Bottom: dace fin concave

Also the mouth is much smaller. Location is not usually difficult, and what applies to roach also applies to dace.

Tackle As for roach, but there is rarely any need to go above a 3 lb. b.s. line.

Tactics Again, mainly as for roach. Many writers, however, describe a bite from a dace as a fast one, but this is not true of good quality fish upwards of 6 oz. or so. When 'trotting', for instance, the bite is a slow, determined one, as it is also when legering at long range. The best bait is generally maggots, or chrysalis, but bread is also good.

GUDGEON Gudgeon are often fished for in all-in matches, but as far as the specimen hunter is concerned their use is for live- or dead-bait. Fine tackle must be used with hooks no larger than a No. 14. The best bait are maggots and brandlings, which are fished on the bottom. Allow the float nearly to disappear before striking. Ground-bait freely with the hook-bait or 'cloud' ground-bait. Failing this, get a long stick or a long-handled garden rake and give the bottom a good stir, for gudgeon are attracted to cloudy water. Often I do not bother with this and merely throw a hand-ful of gravel around the float. Strange to say this does not frighten the fish away.

BLEAK In waters where they abound bleak can be a nuisance, especially in the Thames. Fish fine, using a float carrying one small shot, which is placed about 18 inches above the hook, a No. 16. The best bait is a single maggot, which can be used over and over again. Ground-bait with maggots; failing this a crust of bread thrown on the surface will soon bring the bleak around, and a maggot cast alongside is quickly taken. Fish some 12 inches deep. There is no need to strike, a pull being sufficient.

POPE Never fished for purposely and considered a pest by every-one. Sometimes called a ruff, and very often other names too!

Index